For nearly twenty years David Torrance was a journalist and broadcaster as well as the author and editor of more than a dozen books on Scottish politics and history. He completed a PhD in history and political science in 2017. Like all good Scotsmen, he lives in London, where he is a constitutional specialist at the House of Commons Library.

Lord Clyde
The Orkney Judge

A Biography of James John Clyde
The Rt Hon. the Lord Clyde of Briglands

David Torrance

BIRLINN

First published in Great Britain in 2019 by
Birlinn Ltd
West Newington House
10 Newington Road
Edinburgh
EH9 1QS

www.birlinn.co.uk

ISBN: 978 1 78027 618 2

British Library Cataloguing-in-Publication Data
A catalogue record for this book is available on request
from the British Library

Typeset by Initial Typesetting Services, Edinburgh
Printed and bound by Gutenberg Press, Malta

Contents

List of Plates

Receiving an honorary degree from Heriot-Watt University, 1991

The *Scotsman* front page, 28 October 1992

James when he received an honorary degree from Napier University, 1995

Dublin Street home, the New Town, Edinburgh

The garden at Dublin Street, created by James and Ann

Lord of Appeal in Ordinary, 1996

James with Prince Philip, the Duke of Edinburgh, 1993

Relaxing on holiday

Briglands azaleas in the Shiel garden, 2002

The Shiel garden

Tree planting with his grandson, James 'Moog' Clyde

James's grandchildren, Richard, Charles and James 'Moog' Clyde

James's grandchildren, Quentin and Montague 'Monty' Clyde

James with Tim, Ann and Jamie, 2000

James in his Belfast office as Justice Oversight Commissioner, 2006

James with Ann in the Abercombie Place Gardens, Edinburgh, 2006

Acknowledgements

I would like to thank David Torrance for his patience and dedication in distilling boxes of diaries along with memories of colleagues, friends and family into such a great summary of James's life. I am also very grateful for all the support from my two sons Jamie and Tim. I hope this book will give inspiration to James's five grandsons and the future Clyde generations who were not able to meet and get to know him. He was an exceptional man. I am so fortunate to have been married to him for forty-five very happy years.

Ann Clyde
April 2019

Foreword

by

The Rt Hon. the Lord Mackay of Clashfern KT

I have been honoured to have been invited to write a foreword to this fascinating biography of one of the most distinguished members of the Scottish Bar of his time.

My first acquaintance with the Clyde family was hearing the Lord Advocate participating in a criminal appeal with two other stars of the Bar, John Cameron, then Dean of Faculty, and Ronald Morison. Soon I was to see him again taking his seat as Lord President of the Court of Session when he remarked that notwithstanding the Heritable Jurisdictions (Scotland) Act 1746 he was following his father in taking that chair. In that capacity he welcomed me when I was called to the Bar in 1955 and showed me the greatest kindness.

Shortly after James came to the Bar in 1959 I had been invited by a surveyor in an assessor's office to join him in preparing a new edition of *Armour on Valuation for Rating* to take account of the major changes in that subject brought in by statute in 1956. He was not able to make his contribution and I was delighted when James agreed to join me in this work. To work with James was most congenial and his contribution greatly enhanced the value of the work. It proved a great boon to both of us as the changes generated a large amount of work in the local Committees and in the Valuation Appeal Court.

James's talent as an advocate soon brought him a flourishing practice. Both of us were involved in the Burmah Oil case on opposite sides and had the huge privilege of listening to Sir Milner Holland in the House of Lords and profited from his marvellous advocacy. After I took Silk from time to time I had his support and excellent support it was.

On taking Silk he quickly gained a large practice. With his eye on his family's previous trajectory he entered politics and the biography based on his daily diaries shows the disappointment he experienced. In 1979 to my intense surprise I was invited to be the Lord Advocate. I invited him to rejoin the Crown Office, but he declined. The position of the Scottish Conservative Party in Parliament was the factor that led to this and certainly not any failure to appreciate his merits. In due course he was appointed an Appeal Court judge in Jersey and Guernsey and this brought him into working with senior judges in the English courts. Again he experienced a disappointment in not being appointed to the chair of the Supreme Courts of Scotland but I was delighted in due course to be able to nominate him for appointment as a Lord of Appeal in Ordinary, a member of the Supreme Court of the United Kingdom and of the Judicial Committee of the Privy Council, a position higher than attained by his ancestors. In that position he excelled with many superb judgements.

In all his contacts he was much appreciated by his colleagues often welcomed by his infectious laugh before he could be seen.

He carried out two special responsibilities, one in Orkney and the other in Northern Ireland, in which his outstanding forensic skills, but even more his interpersonal skills and tact, were manifested. To read about this and much more including details of his precious family life, I warmly recommend this well-written biography.

Chapter 1

A Remarkable Academy Family

As a schoolboy, James John Clyde was asked to prepare a mock obituary, presumably as a means of identifying his ambitions and expectations as he prepared to come of age. It began, 'With the death of [the] late Lord President of the Court of Session, Edinburgh has lost an eminent member of the Scottish Bench and Bar', and continued:

> Born in Edinburgh in 1932 he was educated at the Edinburgh Academy. He later studied at Trinity College Oxford and Edinburgh University, as did his father and grandfather. He was called to the Scottish Bar in 1956 and twelve years after he became a K.C. Then he mounted steadily becoming in turn Dean of the Faculty of Advocates, Solicitor-General, Lord Advocate and Lord President of the Court of Session. Being Lord Advocate during this last long period of Conservative government he was returned three times for the Peebles constituency. Many people will recall his speeches in Parliament concerning certain reforms in which he took a special interest.

In 1958 he married Mary the second daughter of Dr Lawson the well-known Dr of Music, and is now survived by her, a son and a daughter. With his keenness for music in Edinburgh he became President of the Edinburgh Music Society and took an important part in the now world-famous Edinburgh Musical Festival which took place each year. His interest in his old school lead [*sic*] him to help the new buildings which he never saw completed. He also advised the building of the great new hall now almost completed at Murrayfield.

When he retired eight years ago from the Scottish Bench, he took up his residence at his country-house at Briglands in Kinrosshire [*sic*]. This house was bought by his grandfather who enlarged it by adding a wing while the grandson extended the gardens and set out a minature [*sic*] lake not far from the house. Nearly all his holidays, or what small portion of rest he had, were spent at his beloved Briglands. Here he lived the last years of his life, often entertaining his friends, for whom his sudden death last night has proved a sad and unexpected bereavement. His most prominent quality was generosity, he gave many large sums of money to help his old school, the Edinburgh Academy, and his name is remembered by the many prizes for art and music which he gave to the school. His interest in his city brought him to rebuild many of the city's houses and lay out the new plans for the new city's gardens.

'Edinburgh', concludes the obituary, 'can never and never shall forget the efforts of the Late Lord Clyde.'

It is clear from James's aspirational essay that he was acutely aware of the achievements of, in his own words, 'his father and grandfather': studies at Oxford and Edinburgh, the Scottish Bar, Dean of the Faculty, Parliament, the Crown Office and, ultimately, becoming Lord President of the Court of Session, as well as hobbies such as music and gardening.

Many of these ambitions, as we shall see, were satisfied, and others were not. Indeed, what James could not have foreseen at that point were the unexpected directions his own career would take, differing from – and in certain respects exceeding – those of his father and grandfather.

Two years before he died in 2009, James John Clyde presented to the Faculty of Advocates what he called 'an imperfectly drafted picture'. Dated 1911, it depicts Parliament Hall with its seventeenth-century hammer-beam roof and advocates – wigged and gowned – pacing the floor in traditional manner. In the foreground are three figures: James's grandfather, James Avon Clyde, a King's Counsel (KC)[1] and Member of Parliament; his wife Anna Margaret McDiarmid; and a young boy gazing up at the roof timbers, James Latham McDiarmid Clyde – James's grandfather, grandmother and father, respectively.

As Lord (Kenneth) Cameron observed in his eulogy at James's memorial service, the gift of this painting 'represented no exorcising of the ghosts of family tradition', for he was understandably proud of the illustrious careers of the first two Lord Clydes, both of whom had become Lord President of the Court of Session in Edinburgh.

By the time James was born at 3 Great Stuart Street, Edinburgh, on 29 January 1932,[2] his grandfather had been Lord President – with the judicial title of Lord Clyde – for twelve years, following terms as Solicitor General for Scotland and, concurrently, Lord Advocate *and* Dean of the Faculty of Advocates. Although James was only twelve when his grandfather died in 1944, others

---

1   Only after the accession of Queen Elizabeth in 1952 did KCs become Queen's Counsels, or QCs.
2   James was baptised at St Mary's Episcopal Cathedral in Edinburgh on 27 February 1932, and later 'confirmed' in the same church.

might have told him of (the first) Lord Clyde's reputation as an outstanding practitioner of Scots Law and a dominant, charismatic figure. 'His appearance, his manner, even his walk,' judged one biographer, 'suggested . . . that he was endowed with an immense store of vitality and power.'

Judging from portraits, James looked a lot like his grandfather: the same sandy-coloured hair; the same kindly expression. However, it was his father, James Latham McDiarmid Clyde, generally known as 'Hamish', who in 1954 would become the second Lord Clyde, who was the dominant figure of his childhood and early adult life. When James John, Hamish's only son, was born in 1932, Hamish was yet to take Silk (that came in 1936), but he had already mirrored his father's CV by attending Edinburgh Academy and studying classics at Oxford.

In 1921, Hamish obtained a third-class degree from Oxford, something redeemed by a pass with distinction in the LLB examination at Edinburgh University three years later. In 1928 he married Margaret Letitia, the daughter of an English barrister called Arthur Edmund DuBuisson. Indeed, the Law – Scottish and English – imbued the broader Clyde clan, Hamish's brother, Richard Arthur Clyde (who trained in England), later founding Clyde & Co., a firm of City solicitors which still bore his name in the early twenty-first century.[3]

James John's childhood was rooted in two places, the elegant surroundings of Edinburgh's Georgian New Town and Briglands at Rumbling Bridge in Kinross-shire, a small country estate the first Lord Clyde had acquired at the turn of the twentieth century, literally 'to cultivate his garden' (a horticultural passion later continued by his grandson). As James would reflect in 2008, members of the Clyde family were resident at Heriot Row for most of the twentieth century, his grandfather

---

3   Today, Clyde & Co. employs more than 3,000 staff in more than forty locations on six continents.

at No. 17 (once home to the writer and advocate Robert Louis Stevenson), his father at No. 14 and him at No. 5 and then No. 9.

The Clyde family moved to No. 14 shortly after James was born, and would remain there for the next forty years. He and his elder sister Ann were 'quartered' on the first floor, from which a stone staircase led to the upper floor, 'presumably designed', as he later recalled, so that 'the children could be neither seen nor heard'. 'There was a flat roof with a stair leading to it off the landing,' James also recalled, 'and we used to adventure up there to sit in the sunshine.' He also had clear memories of gas lamplighters, a man with a 'hurdy-gurdy machine' who played in the street for a living, and horse-drawn vehicles (including a milk lorry) clattering along road surfaces of stone setts.

The front gardens, for the exclusive use of residents, were a favourite play area for James and Ann, where they sailed toy boats on the pond and rode bicycles 'at high speeds' around the paths. No. 14 being a large house, James's parents employed a cook/housekeeper called Margaret Macfadyen, a Gaelic speaker from Mull. She lived in the basement where, during the war, the family would retire when the air-raid siren sounded. James remembered walking up and down the stairs 'at least half asleep', and also a bucket of sand and 'a stirrup pump operated by hand whose little trickle of water was intended to extinguish a fire'. Luckily, that never proved necessary, although they did once find a piece of shrapnel on the roof.

James's sister Ann also remembered them playing together at Briglands, making skis and building boats from planks of wood. 'There was a nasty little pond in the woods,' she recalled, 'just a mud hole really, and we got our boat – which was just planks of wood nailed together – but it wouldn't float and it went down! There was no main road near Briglands, so it was a good place to play. We used to go for bicycle rides and picnics – it had a lovely great big garden and grounds.'

Gathering clouds in Europe warranted compromises, and for a while a naval officer was billeted with the Clydes. The 1938 Munich Crisis (in which Neville Chamberlain vainly attempted to appease Hitler) delayed the opening of term at Edinburgh Academy by a week. It was in October that year James 'came' to the school. His great-grandfather, Dr James Clyde, 'a classical scholar with a European reputation', had taught there, while James's grandfather had been Dux of the school in 1880, as was his father in 1916.

The war, when it came, took its toll on the school, with many boys evacuated (the school roll practically halved) and the staff decimated, with the Scottish Education Department even having to provide a grant to keep it afloat financially, meaning the Academy temporarily suspended its 'independence'. The boys, meanwhile, dug trenches in New Field, built air-raid shelters and rehearsed getting under cover, and when the sirens sounded they were marched down to basement shelters. The Academy also accepted six Austrian refugees, and later eight Poles, giving James and his fellow pupils their first experience of European diversity.

James's schooldays are particularly well documented, for in 1938 he also began to keep a journal – initially more of a scrapbook – encouraged by his mother to maintain a record of his life, which he was to continue for his whole life. The first volume opens with pages 'from an autograph book' dated 1938, sketches by 'MLC' (James's mother), a page assembled at Briglands (also in 1938) and a quote from Longfellow, which captured something, perhaps, of the motivation behind such a record:

> The heights by great men reached and kept
> were not attained by sudden flight,
> But they, while their companions slept,
> Were toiling upward in the night.

But this was a false start, for the Clyde Archive only begins in earnest in 1944, when the Edinburgh Academy roll for that session records James as being in Class III and 'House Car' (Carmichael). Early essays included 'Places of Interest in Edinburgh' and another entitled 'My School'. 'School starts at 9 o'clock and continues till 3,' he wrote, observing wryly: 'The discipline has fallen with the war so all the boys are not as good as gold.'

On 1 January 1946, James also started keeping a daily diary, a habit he would maintain for the next sixty-three years. Without fail these entries – usually quite brief – would begin with a description of the weather, thus in his first, on a Tuesday, he recorded:

> Bitterly cold. White frost. Failed to sledge. Played and broke ice on pond and river. Plum pudding for dinner.

Some time later James took the trouble of typing up these early entries, adding a retrospective commentary in parentheses. Prompted by the memory of plum pudding at the beginning of 1946, he recalled: 'This would be the remains of the pudding served on Christmas Day, which was usually finished up on New Year's Day.'

Thereafter the diaries record three main areas of James's early life: the arts, politics and his broader personal development, all of which revolved around Edinburgh Academy, indeed the first of those – chiefly music and theatre – dominates his early journals and scrapbooks. One early diary entry records the Theatre Royal burning down and him going to 'see [the] remains after lunch'.

There must have been a youthful desire to tread the boards (he was a regular visitor to Edinburgh's theatres and cinemas) for in the mid-to-late 1940s James played Lady Capulet in the Dramatic Society's production of *Romeo and Juliet*, Miss Ada Shore in James Bridie's *What Say They?* and the Duke of Albany in *King Lear*, a performance the Edinburgh Academy *Chronicle* believed 'stood out with earnestness and authority against the iniquities of his towering queen'. On 2 October 1947

James recorded in his diary that 'M[agnus] Magnusson' (later a prominent journalist and broadcaster) 'asked me to join the Play-Reading Society', and by 1950 he had become its secretary.

But his main preoccupation was clearly musical, with two outings in Gilbert and Sullivan operas allowing James to combine that with his interest in theatre. First, he played Josephine (the Captain's daughter) in *HMS Pinafore* towards the end of the war, and then Dame Hannah in *Ruddigore* in 1947. Of his latter performance, the *Chronicle* noted that 'if under strain on the top notes in Act I', James then redeemed himself with 'that lovely Sullivan duet, "The Great Oak Tree," the two voices blending with peculiar sweetness'. He also made an impact on his younger contemporaries. David Hope (later Lord Hope), who was a few years behind James at the Academy, clearly recalls at least one of these. 'He was very debonair,' he remembered, 'a distant hero really.' Similarly, even several decades later, Robin Bell, a future legal contemporary and neighbour, could remember James singing 'My Little Buttercup' dressed, of course, as a girl.

James loved music, both singing and playing the cello and organ, for which prizes flowed. In 1944, he won the Ernest R. Balfour Music Prize for singing (along with seven others, including Magnus Magnusson), and in 1946, 1947 and 1948 there were further accolades for singing, cello playing, or both. In May 1947, the school also gave him permission to play in the Edinburgh Musical Festival in the 'cello under 18' category; he recorded with pride in his diary that he 'was the only entrant and got 86%'. James also composed music. A school contemporary later reminded him of listening to a string quartet he had written to which, with characteristic modesty, he replied: 'It was only a string trio!'

It might have been this to which the *Chronicle* referred as a 'unique' performance, a cello solo in one of James's 'own compositions' called 'Andante Cantabile'. He performed it at the Academy's Musical Society on 24 February 1950, and also entered it into the Edinburgh Festival Competition Prize but did not win. 'I hope it is playable!' he had written in his diary a few days before the performance, having spent all day making a 'fair copy' of his work. Later that year the *Chronicle* also gave James a good write-up for his and N. L. Lawrie's performance of the first movement from Mozart's Symphony No. 41 in C major (the 'Jupiter'). The review said that:

> one or two slight flaws apart it had all the assurance one expected of two such accomplished musicians, and it is no reflection on Clyde's competence as a pianist to say that one felt a little wistful for his 'cello. The performance of the two young pianists gave encouraging hope for the future: they both played their pieces with notable intelligence and control, and for the very occasional note that failed to come through the fault lay not with the performer's technique but with the unusual depth of touch on that particular vintage of Broadwood grand.

Doubtless James would have taken considerable satisfaction at this recognition of his abilities as a pianist, indeed he would try to improve his theoretical and practical mastery of that instrument for another six decades.

James was not, however, at all interested in sport, and particularly disliked having to play rugby at school. Later a friend, Sandy Wilkinson, remembered that if James said of an acquaintance that he was 'a rugger player', then 'one knew that it was not a compliment'. His interests, as was befitting a future judge and Law Lord, were more cerebral and spiritual. As a boy, he attended All Saints in Tollcross and also Old St Paul's in Edinburgh's Old Town (where he would later play the organ). James's faith was doubtless influenced by his mother, who took such things very seriously, unlike his father.

Although politics did not capture James's imagination in quite the same way, it is clear from his early diaries and papers that

he followed current affairs and anticipated following both his
father and grandfather into Parliament. Like most advocates in
those days his father took an active part in politics, first con-
testing the general election that followed the end of the Second
World War. Among James's papers is his father's modest calling
card, 'Requesting the favour of your support on Polling Day,
5th July', although the election actually took place on 12 July
1945. Hamish Clyde, however, failed to become the Member
for Peebles and Southern Midlothian (the constituency James
had predicted representing himself), coming a poor second to
the successful Labour candidate.[4]

James enjoyed disputation – lively, congenial debate – and
in October 1946 he attended a meeting of the United Nations
Association at the Usher Hall, where he heard the future
Conservative Prime Minister Harold Macmillan speak and the
Reverend S. Harvie Clark read out the preamble to the UN
Charter, which had been signed the previous June. Earlier that
year he had also been at the Usher Hall for the annual conference of the Scottish Unionist Association (which was how
the Conservative Party then styled itself north of the border), as
well as another Unionist gathering in Peebles, with his father, in
February 1947.

At that time, the Labour Party dominated Scottish and British
politics, Clement Attlee having succeeded Winston Churchill
as Prime Minister in 1945. Scottish Nationalism also loomed
large in the late 1940s, although of the variety that agitated for
a devolved Scottish Parliament rather than outright independence. James was likely a cynic, for when, in November 1949,
the Academy's Debating Society discussed the motion that 'A
Scottish Parliament is compatible with the natural growth of

---

4   James's grandfather had served as Liberal Unionist MP for Edinburgh
    West, winning the seat at a by-election in 1909 and holding it until
    1918, after which he was the Coalition Unionist MP for Edinburgh
    North until 1920.

the British Commonwealth', he was opposed, scorning the notion that a Scotland with its own parliament would continue to co-operate with England. 'Look at Southern Ireland!' he said gloomily. He lost the debate, as he later noted in his diary, by 13 votes to 17.

In another debate in October 1950, on the motion 'That democracy is a failure', James proposed an 'alternative to the present system', suggesting that political parties be removed and candidates instead elected 'because of their characters'. This was youthful idealism, although under the existing electoral system his father had recently become the Scottish Unionist MP for North Edinburgh. Indeed prior to the general election, James had accompanied his 'Da and Ma' (as he usually referred to them) to a rally addressed by Winston Churchill, again at the Usher Hall, and watched as his father, not yet an MP, 'made [a] very successful vote of thanks'.

Curiously, the Law does not intrude very often, at least judging by James's school diaries and papers. In July 1949, he records lunch with the Maxwell Fyfes (David having been the lead prosecutor at the Nuremberg Trials) and, earlier that year, going to Parliament House with his father to listen to some cases, but beyond that there is little indication of interest in his father's profession, although perhaps so prevalent was the assumption he too would become a lawyer that it barely required mentioning.

But what is clear was James's commitment to education. In an essay entitled 'What is Education?', he observed that 'education is the development of the whole character, that is body, mind and spirit . . . the teaching of what is good and honourable and what is not'; a 'true education' he believed would be 'continuous all through life till death'. Even so, James initially found his schooling hard-going and often dull, something reflected in early progress reports. One for the 1937–38 session, for example, had predicted that when 'he succeeds in overcoming his fear

of school and of his fellows he should do quite well, but meantime his work is bound to be affected by his many emotional
upheavals at home'.

This was probably a reference to James's childhood eczema,
an unpleasant condition that warranted several consultations
with a skin specialist, as well as long absences from the Academy.
At Prep School his work was generally good but did not show
'much individuality', according to another report, while in the
1941–42 session the class mistress was still urging 'more independence and greater self-reliance'. Only when James reached
the Upper School did matters seem to improve, with his 1946
report noting that he was 'steadily increasing in self-confidence',
perhaps helped by his obvious talent for musical performance
and promotion in January that year in the school's Officer
Training Corps (OTC). The word 'groo' or 'grooey' fea-
tures a lot in early diary entries, which seems to have been an
expression of disapproval, a variation on the more conventional
'boo'.

In 1946 James also started learning to drive, his mother
allowing him to motor back to Edinburgh from Briglands one
day in April, although this did not go entirely to plan. 'Ma was
showing me how to drive on the way back,' he later recorded in
his diary. 'Trying to slow down at one stage I trod too heavily
on the foot brake and a car following behind almost ran into
us, and then swung past, furious. Ma then took over the wheel.'
Nevertheless, in the summer of 1948 James would receive his
first driver's licence from Edinburgh Burgh Council.

In the 1947 session, James made a model of a Roman camp
which later became a permanent exhibit at the Academy, while
in the summer of 1948 another report noted that he was still
'gaining confidence and independence', so much so that by that
Christmas one of his teachers concluded that he had already
'made up his mind about the nature and destiny of man'.
'History has no lessons for him,' they added. 'Secure in his own
convictions (some might call them prejudices) he stands firmly

facing the past. We shall see.' By the following year, however, James was approaching matters 'with a more open mind', and in the 1950–51 session he truly began to excel, serving as a school 'Ephor' (taken from the Greek), or prefect, and winning the Clyde and Millar Greek Prize (co-founded by his relative) jointly with another pupil.

By that point, James was preparing for the next phase of his life. On 4 March 1950, his diary records him registering at Tollcross Labour Exchange and arranging deferment from National Service, then mandatory for every boy of his age. Later that year he got his entry form for a scholarship at Oxford University but was clearly in two minds. 'Oh dear. Should I do my military service first?' he wrote on 24 October, clearly deciding against for two days later he dispatched his application form but forgot, as he also recorded in his diary, 'the testimonial of good character – panic!'

It clearly did not make any difference, for on 4 December 1950 James found himself travelling to Oxford by train to sit several 'terrible' papers while staying in rooms at Merton College. The following day he was 'full of despondency', while on 7 December he was in a 'dead panic about [the] interview'. Again, there was no cause for concern, for on 10 January 1951 his diary notes with obvious excitement: 'Got telegram from Corpus saying I have SCHOLARSHIP!!! Oh cheers!!!'

But there were still several months of schooling to complete. In May 1951, James proposed – and won – the Debating Society motion that 'the Edinburgh International Festival is not a festival of music and drama but a festival of snobbery' and, on 31 July, wrote up his last day at school rather matter-of-factly in his diary: 'Exhibition. I got Dux Medal.' As Lord Mackintosh, chairman of the Academy directors, said, this represented 'a truly remarkable record' without parallel either in the school's history, or indeed that of any other school. 'Third Clyde Is Academy Dux' was a headline in the *Chronicle*, which noted the 'striking example both of the legal and family traditions of the

Academy', for James John Clyde was 'the third of his family in direct succession to attain to the distinction'.

Following James's academic triumph, which must have been all the more satisfying given his uncertain start at the school, it was all change. 'George' Seaman, Rector during James's years at the Academy, retired, while, as his diary also recorded on 31 July 1951, James 'went off to camp at Garelochhead'. By now a platoon sergeant-major in the Combined Cadet Force (CCF), he had also been awarded the Ozanne Cup for the best-kept tent at the CCF camp.[5]

There were also changes at home in Heriot Row, where James's sister, having left home as early as possible, had married Michael Butler, later Sir Michael, a diplomat and early supporter of European integration. In 1951 their father, a dominant figure described by Sir David Edward as 'rarely at rest', was soon to be appointed Lord Advocate, following, as his son would have been aware, a career path already trodden by his grandfather. Blessed with loving and caring (if also strict and demanding) parents, James's path seemed set: having honoured the family tradition by becoming Dux of Edinburgh Academy, he was now preparing for university life. As Magnus Magnusson later observed in his history of James's *alma mater*, *The Clacken and the Slate*: 'Yes, a remarkable Academy family, the Clydes.'

5　Other prizes James received that day were the Clyde and Millar Greek Prize (again), the Rector's Prize for Reading in Hall, and, also not for the first time, the Ernest R. Balfour Music Prize.

Chapter 2

Captain Clyde

James started at Oxford in October 1951, sharing rooms at Corpus Christi with another new student called J. H. Whale, although also at the university were familiar faces from Edinburgh Academy such as Magnus Magnusson and Kenneth (or Kenny) Cameron, who would become a close friend. 'Both at school and at Corpus he was a noted musician and actor,' recalled Cameron several decades later, adding that he 'was not a sportsman'. 'At Corpus he occasionally ploughed his way through the fields of mud that passed at that time for the North Oxford Golf Course, indeed, he claimed that on one occasion he was invited to represent the college at golf but was saved by the cancellation of the match through the death of King George.'

That would date James's lucky escape to February 1952, prior to which his diaries do indeed record a whirlwind of choir practice, amateur dramatics, tea and, whatever his limitations, golf. Shortly after he arrived amid the dreaming spires of Oxford there was also a significant development at home in Edinburgh. 'Ma and Da rang up,' he recorded in his diary on 2 November 1951. 'DA IS LORD ADVOCATE!!!' Already a Member of Parliament, James's father was now a Privy Councillor and member of Winston Churchill's second (and last) government. In March 1952, he dined with his parents at the House of Commons, thereafter staying with his godfather Uncle

Dick (of the City law firm Clyde & Co.) at his home on Dorset Street, something he described in his diary as 'a brief spell of freedom'.

Otherwise, musical and theatrical pursuits dominated James's first couple of years as an undergraduate. In September 1951, he had taken part in the Corpus (whose dramatic society was known as The Owlets) production of T. S. Eliot's *Murder in the Cathedral*, which included performances at Arbroath Abbey, St Andrews and St Giles' Cathedral during the 1952 Edinburgh International Festival (he would also play 'the Messenger' in a revival exactly fifty years later with the same cast). That same summer, James composed and directed the music for an Oxford University Dramatic Society (OUDS) production of *Twelfth Night*, described by one reviewer as 'unportentous and harmless'. He received a better write-up for his musical work on Büchner's *Woyzeck*, a composition the *Pelican Record* praised as 'brilliantly evocative – by turns frightening and beguiling and always apt'.

The summer of 1953 was particularly eventful. On 2 June, James got up at 5am and had breakfast with his parents at the House of Commons. He and Kenny Cameron then stood on Bridge Street between 8am and 2pm to watch the Coronation procession and listen to the service at Westminster Abbey relayed over loudspeakers, during which it rained heavily (unknown to him, he stood only yards from his future wife Ann, who had also decided to watch the procession on Westminster Bridge). Then it was back to Parliament for lunch with his parents on the Commons Terrace (they had champagne to celebrate), on to the Mall to catch the return procession, and finally sight of the Queen and the Duke of Edinburgh at 9.45pm. 'Kenneth and I went to Whitehall Court – Sheriff somebody's flat', James later wrote in his diary, 'and watched superb South Bank fireworks at 10.30 to 11.30. Spent night with Kenneth's aunt in S. Kensington. Bed after 1.0!!!'

A week or so later James spotted a car 'out [on] the Cowley

Road' and telephoned his parents for advice. 'They say buy,' he noted in his diary. 'What shall I do? Think I will.' On 16 June, another brief diary note revealed his decision: 'Bought the Morris 8 1940 tourer, £295!!!'

On 19 June, James had an interview at the War Office (having attended its Selection Board in Andover a few months earlier), while a few days after that he was in Edinburgh to watch the new monarch and her consort's 'State Entry into Edinburgh – from the balcony of the New Club'. His mother went to the Holyrood Presentation Party that evening, and the following day both his parents attended a garden party (and later a dinner party) at Holyrood Palace 'where they chatted with the Queen and the Duke'. Finally, on 27 June, James watched as Queen Elizabeth received the keys to Edinburgh Castle.

In July 1953, James was informed he had been accepted for National Service (NS) Commissions in the Intelligence Corps, although this was deferred until the following year, giving him time to finish his degree. He had, of course, no choice but to serve, and the prospect of several years in the Army clearly did not fill him with elation, particularly after such an enjoyable summer. After his final year of studies James had his NS medical exam, although he was rated Grade 3 due to his eczema. In a diary annotation added a decade later, he remembered being 'quite frightened' that this would mean not being called up at all, something that 'seemed at the time so much worse a fate than to spend two years soldiering'. But he was subsequently upgraded, 'quite arbitrarily', and on 22 July 1954 he writes sadly: 'I got my call up papers – today fortnight. Oh dear.'

Just over a week later he caught the train back to Oxford with his parents and, 'according to custom', had sherry with the president of the college before his degree ceremony at the Sheldonian Theatre, something James described as 'as cursory as could be imagined'. He got a good second-class degree in *literae humaniores* (beating his grandfather's third from Trinity), otherwise known as 'Greats'. His parents photographed the new graduate and then took him for dinner and to see a play in London. 'What a long day,' James later reflected. 'I can't believe I've been back to Oxford. All so sudden, and brief.' Shortly after that he described a day spent in London watching cinema news-reels and wandering the streets. 'When will I be civilised again?' he wondered.

James joined the Army on 5 August 1954 at Blenheim Barracks near Aldershot. His initiation 'included much form filling, an oath, [and] a ruthless haircut', while sleeping accommodation had twenty men to a room, each with a bed and a locker. He had, in his own description, 'toiled' in the Oxford University Training Corps and also completed eight weeks' training at Catterick in order to avoid doing it all over again on being called up, but for whatever reason he did not, as planned, progress straight to an Officer Cadet Training Unit. There followed, therefore, days of drill and kit cleaning.

A month later James finally made it to Eaton Hall (the Officer Cadet School), home to the Duke of Westminster. The Duchess still inhabited part of the massive building, but even amid more agreeable surroundings the adjective 'dull' punctuates his diary entries. He did his best to keep up a routine – as he had at school and university – attending chapel, playing the organ and attending the cinema or theatre whenever possible. He was paid £10 every two weeks.

Earlier that summer James had watched his father receive an honorary Doctor of Laws degree from the University of Edinburgh, perhaps unaware that further accolades were to follow. Towards the end of 1954, Hamish was appointed Lord Justice-General and Lord President of the Court of Session in succession to the legendary Lord Cooper, and installed with the judicial title of Lord Clyde (like his father before him) in January 1955. James was clearly proud of his father, for one carefully compiled volume of his papers opens with photographs of the new Lord President alongside his son in Army uniform.

The same month his father became the second Lord Clyde, James was commissioned into the Intelligence Corps and posted to Mansfield Camp on 16 January. Following another routine few months, he learned he was to be posted to Nicosia, then capital of the British colony of Cyprus, but when he turned up at Goodge Street Deep Shelter on 20 June he found his plane was actually due to leave the following evening. The flight took all night and stopped at Naples en route, 'flying past Vesuvius as the sun began to rise'. It reached Nicosia at 9am on 22 June. 'I was shown my room – small, and very hot,' James wrote in his diary, 'with terrifying insects rattling around the floor or flying about the air.' Just a day later he was surprised to learn he might soon be transferred to Egypt and indeed, several mosquito bites later, he flew there on 19 July. 'Fighting has begun in Gaza,' he recorded on 22 August 1955, 'trouble in the Sudan – thrill for us.'

At one point James was hospitalised in Moascar, prompting him to send a postcard (of himself) to his sister Ann, by then married to Michael Butler (diplomat) and living in New York and Baghdad. 'This is me just after I came out of Hospital,' he wrote apologetically. 'This may explain some of the awfulness of the picture [he looked very thin]. The rest must be my inanity. Please hide it somewhere Anyway, it's the thought that counts, and this is with my VERY best wishes for Christmas, James.'

Despite the jocular tone of communications such as this, lack of self-confidence continued to plague James, just as it had at Edinburgh Academy. On 24 October, he wrote about 'a terrible day. Disaster after disaster', convinced that his troop sergeant had 'no confidence' in him. 'Absolutely miserable,' he added bleakly, 'I feel an utter failure.' This feeling, however, was clearly misplaced, for on 4 November James 'emerged as Captain Clyde'. Although he had gone to Egypt to help wind down the British Army presence there, the independence and character of his daily intelligence reports had warranted the unusual promotion (as a National Serviceman) from second lieutenant to the rank of temporary captain.

On 20 November, James went for a day trip to Cairo, seeing 'all the obvious tourist spots' and, on 6 December, flew back to Cyprus ('Horrid trip'). Opting not to return home that Christmas, he later recalled a plague of locusts that appeared out of the blue one day, settling in their 'hundreds over the compound, creatures about 6 inches long'. In spite of such Biblical scenes, James seemed to be enjoying his National Service a little more, writing approvingly of 'tree-lined roads . . . where I would walk every Sunday morning, the magnificent flame-coloured flowers [lining] the Mall . . . the church, the shops, the open-air cinema which I never attended. Ismailia with its traffic, its shops, its trees and gardens.'

Nevertheless, the first few months of 1956 appear to have been quite dull, enlivened only by a classical music club (at which James could play gramophone records), bridge and the occasional dinner. On 24 April, however, he flew to Amman in Jordan, where General Headquarters had much better mess facilities, as well as the opportunity to view some of the historical sites he had read about at Oxford. For example, on 19 May, James visited Jerash, something he described with obvious pleasure as 'a wonderful, wonderful day'. His diary continues:

> After a fairly long drive we reached Jerash and spent the middle of the day walking around and through it. Gracious what a place! With two theatres in remarkably good repair. While we were at one of them a little boy offered to sell us some old coins, found on the site. I bought two. We had a sandwich lunch there in the forum, which is a large oval in shape, paved with huge flat stones and surrounded by a lofty colonnade, much of which stands.

The following month he also went to Petra for the day. 'And what indescribable beauty,' he wrote in his diary. 'Didn't see everything but had a wonderful time; the "Treasury" turning a rich red as we left, the ride through the gorge unbelievable.' On another trip, James also saw the Dead Sea, Jericho, Jerusalem and Bethlehem. 'Cannot describe what I felt,' he reflected later. 'Very rushed and main impression is of unhappiness and worry, though Jerusalem seems somehow peaceful.'

Indeed the Middle East of the mid 1950s was notoriously unstable, the Suez Crisis just weeks away. 'I hear there was a change of government in Jordan two days ago (and although we are in the country we had heard nothing of it!),' James noted in his diary on 22 May. 'Wonder if trouble is brewing.' But despite the aesthetic pleasures of Jordan, James's mood continued to fluctuate. Towards the end of the month, for example, he wrote of 'another dismal day': 'Oh dear. I feel very much cut off from home. Why don't they tell me to go?'

Go he did on 13 June, flying back to Cyprus where he caught an Army production of Gilbert and Sullivan's *Pirates of Penzance*. 'I see I am billed as Assistant Producer,' he mused in his diary: 'Heavens!' Later that month he also sat a music exam, the examiners having dispatched the relevant material to Cyprus; James did 'very badly' on one paper but passed the other. In a long typewritten letter home on 17 June, he lamented the 'sticky heat' and a deterioration in the security situation, Famagusta beach 'now a controlled area, wired off and guarded'. James also thought out loud about the following six weeks, talking about returning to the UK via Italy, or possibly via Beirut, from which he hoped to visit Damascus and Baalbek, 'which I think will COMPLETE my record of Middle East sites'.

'What a two years it has been,' he reflected more generally. 'Or at least what a last year it has been. There are bits that seem so fantastic that I can't believe that it was really me. I'm sure I'm not really the right sort of person for the part.' James also wrote of having recently defended someone in a court martial, having done another that spring, a useful (if stressful) experience for a future advocate.

There was further drama to come, for on 23 June, while

staying with a Major Beard at his home on Hercules Street in Famagusta, there was a terrorist attack. As James's diary records:

> I never heard the faint tinkle of one of the car window's [*sic*] breaking, but everyone else had leapt up at once and rushed out of the room. I found my weapon and followed. The bombs were made of petrol in a bottle with some kind of fuse and served as quite efficient incendiaries. As we ran out by the side door (the car had been parked in the side street) we heard running footsteps in the street out at the front but by the time we had got out of the door and round the corner there was no culprit to be seen.

In a separate account written years later, James recalled it as 'all quite a bizarre experience, but exciting'. 'My main feeling was a thirst to get at the culprit and a disappointment that we had not succeeded in catching anyone.' Decades later, according to his legal contemporary and friend Robin Bell, James got talking to a Greek Cypriot lawyer at a legal conference in Cyprus and realised that 'this fellow had been doing the firing all those years before, but typically James didn't mention that he'd been in the Army or in Cyprus – he was very discreet'.

His studies having been interrupted by two years of National Service, on returning to Scotland James's priority was to complete his education – and of course facilitate his future career – with a degree in law at the University of Edinburgh, just as his father and grandfather had done. Meanwhile, he slipped back into his old routine of golf, trips to Briglands, visits to the Edinburgh Festival, music and spending time with his parents at Heriot Row, where his childhood home had recently been redecorated. The city of his youth was also changing, and on 11 November James wrote of 'probably my last trip on an Edinburgh tram'.

Nevertheless, it must have been a welcome dose of nor-
mality following the heat and stresses of the Middle East. On
3 October 1956, James matriculated at Edinburgh University
and began his studies a few days later, although later that month
he noted in his diary the beginning of what became known
as the Suez Crisis: 'Middle East has blown up most interestingly – Israel invading Egypt.' He had missed a historic event
– one that humiliated British foreign policy – by a matter of
months.

James excelled at his studies, gaining several certificates of
merit after his first year at Edinburgh, as well as securing the
Thow Scholarship in Civil Law, Constitutional Law and Public
Law (which was considered important enough to merit a mention in the *Scotsman*). Robin Bell recalls 'being very cross' that
his fellow student 'swept the board' with all the big legal prizes.
Sandy Wilkinson was more charitable in saying that James 'was
a student of clearly exceptional ability and would, I think, generally be regarded as the most outstanding of the Edinburgh Law
graduates of 1959'. 'Although not gregarious,' he added, 'he was
sociable, enjoyed the company of his friends, participated in
law-related extra-mural activities.'

James's father's status as Lord President also guaranteed a
range of stimulating visitors at Heriot Row. In August 1957,
for example, Chief Justice Earl Warren of the United States
came to see 'Da' and they all had sherry before dinner. 'He was
a big man,' recorded James in his diary, 'kind and charming.'
Best known for ending racial segregation in American schools,
Warren had also served (three times) as Governor of California
and would later lead an investigation into the assassination of John
F. Kennedy.

James threw himself into a range of activities expected
of any ambitious law student. Not only was he active in the
Edinburgh University Law Society, but in October 1957 he was
introduced to the prestigious Speculative Society, in which his
grandfather had also learned to debate, as well as serving as its

librarian and president (1959–60).[1] Contemporaries at 'the Spec' included Nicholas Fairbairn and James's friend Kenny Cameron, who served as secretary in its 1958–59 session and president in 1959–60. He also joined the Diagnostic Society but considered it 'a poor copy of the Spec' and later resigned, devoting more of his energy to the coveted *Scotsman* Debating Trophy in 1958 and 1959.

On 1 October 1957, James started work as an 'apprentice' at Macpherson & Mackay WS, one of the busiest offices in Edinburgh when it came to court work, as he later reflected, 'and consequently the most suitable training-ground for the Bar'. The structure of legal education in those days was very different from that in the early twenty-first century. For prospective solicitors, study for the LLB degree was combined with a three-year apprenticeship with a legal firm or, for prospective advocates, a two-year 'bar apprenticeship' followed by a year 'devilling' for an advocate. This practice ceased in 1960, making James's generation one of the last to learn the ropes in such a way.

The resulting time pressures on students (and on the curriculum) meant that James and his colleagues ended up taking a generalist approach to their studies rather than developing a deeper interest in particular areas of law. James spent his time at Macpherson & Mackay working with three partners (two of whom dealt with the courts) at an office on Melville Street at the West End of the New Town. It was there he first met his lifelong friend Sandy Wilkinson, later a sheriff. 'Although we came from very different backgrounds, our friendship developed very quickly,' he recalled. 'His sense of humour impressed me from the start: it was subtle, allusive, usually gentle but sometimes, in an allusive way, quite pointed.'

---

1   In the third published history of 'the Spec', James is listed as member 1688, 'son of 1403; grandson of 1131'.

Between 9am and 5pm Monday–Friday were the 'official hours of work' at Macpherson & Mackay, although for most of his time there James also worked every other Saturday (in the summer months this became *every* Saturday). However, the apprentices' hours were shorter as they had lectures in the morning and some evenings, so James and the others would arrive at around 11.30am and leave at 3.30pm in order to make their 4pm class.

There was, as James later recorded in an aide memoire, a lot of 'routine work', copying counsel's adjustments to written pleadings, amending records, inventories, and so on, much of which took place at Register House, one of the most 'tiresome' tasks being to copy the interlocutor sheets (containing formal minutes of court decisions), first at Register House and then again into a large loose-leaf book back at Melville Street. 'This kind of work was instructive to a certain extent,' James observed wryly, 'but once the drill was learnt – which did not take very long – I felt that as far as it was concerned the office was profiting a great deal more out of my services than I was benefiting by the experience.'

He enjoyed much more the drawing up of legal aid memoranda and applications to the Law Society of Scotland for assistance in raising an action, usually for divorce proceedings. Occasionally he would even get to leave the office and take a precognition from witnesses for a case, once paying 'a memorable visit to a slum in Leith and a steel foundry in search for information'. He also spent a lot of time at Parliament House. 'The worst job here was dealing with our witnesses when we had a proof or a trial,' he recalled. 'They had to be fed at lunchtime, kept tolerably happy, and stationed at the proper place when they were due to be called.'

Macpherson & Mackay, James remembered, 'had a cheerful atmosphere about it, and no one was very strict,' while the memory of one of the partner's typists, 'a vivacious young woman with an accent as hard as nails,' stayed with him not least because 'she hammered at her machine at a most fearsome speed' that he 'wondered how the poor thing didn't fall to pieces in her hands'. Emma (he never learned her surname) was also one of the few typists in the office who would dare answer back to Mr Stewart (the partner) while he was giving dictation.

Frustratingly for James, his work was unpaid because a 'tremendous battle' with the Ministry of Pensions and National Insurance meant it was easier (and cheaper) for the firm to class him as an unpaid apprentice, while others received £75 a year. 'The normal apprenticeship which a prospective solicitor undergoes is three years long,' James reflected on leaving Macpherson & Mackay in June 1958. 'I have only been with M & M for half that period, but I hope that I have learnt enough from the experience for my purposes, and while I am in some ways sorry to be leaving it, the future prospect seems attractive.'[2]

On 1 January 1958, James had noted having 'kept a diary now for eleven years, so far always in little printed books'. 'Now,' he added, 'I am starting in this new form,' which was to be handwritten un-ruled pages of foolscap. These continued to record the weather and his daily activities, and quite often captured his irreverent sense of humour. 'The Duke of Hamilton rang up, asking for Ma, and I took the call,' he wrote on 3 January. 'What do you call a Duke on the telephone?'

James also used his diary to record the inauguration of the actor James Robertson Justice as Rector of Edinburgh University on 20 February (he briefly glimpsed the Duke of Edinburgh outside the McEwan Hall), summer travels in the Highlands and more accolades, including the MacLagan Prize in Forensic Medicine in July of that year. He had been devilling to Jack Mackenzie Stuart (later Lord Mackenzie-Stuart, a judge and president of the European Court of Justice), that is, working

---

2   James had actually worked at Macpherson & Mackay for less than a year.

alongside a qualified advocate as his 'devil' or trainee, and the final step in the process of being called to the Scottish Bar in his own right. This particular association would also imbue James with a subsequent interest in the European project and its legal implications.

By the June of 1959, however, James's thoughts turned to practical matters ahead of his graduation. He arranged for an offer to be made on a basement flat at No. 5 Heriot Row, and when the owner decided to sell rather than rent it, he offered £4,000 to secure it. As the flat was being decorated James started clearing out his room at No. 14. On 13 July, he graduated in law with distinction, also being awarded the Vans Dunlop Scholarship in Conveyancing at his graduation ceremony in the McEwan Hall.

Just days later, James also took a private examination for entry into the Faculty of Advocates, donning a tail coat, white tie and stiff-collared shirt. 'After a wait [we] were ushered into a room off the library corridor where we handed over our degree certificates, withdrew, returned, to be told that we had satisfied the examiners of our credentials and that was that,' he wrote in his diary on 17 July. 'I was asked what the subject of my Oxford B.A. degree was, but otherwise the affair was a formality.'

Then, on 24 July 1959, James was called to the Scottish Bar at Parliament House, or in the time-honoured phrase 'passed advocate', once again waiting in a room off the library corridor in evening dress. This traditional rite of passage required the entrant to present, and be examined upon, a Latin thesis on Roman Law, a tradition, as Kenny Cameron later mused, 'more honoured in the breach than in the observance', for cribbing from a nineteenth- or even eighteenth-century thesis was commonplace.

James's thesis, however, was an original one, and contained a phrase which encapsulated a principle that would underpin his whole life in the Law, be it as a counsel, QC or judge: *eis qui servitutem nobis machinantur usque ad extremum spiritum resistimus* ('we should resist to our last breath those who seek to enslave us'), an expression of abhorrence of tyranny of any kind, personal or state inspired. As James himself recorded in his diary: 'I was first, went in, bowed and was handed my thesis by the Dean and asked to read my first aemeseum.'

> There were about 20 members of the Faculty present. I did so, [Jack] Mackenzie Stuart rattled off the question which I had given him and I replied. Then the second and third ammena, with questions by Duffes Q.C. and Gordon Coutts. The question and answers had been prepared by me earlier in the week and I had distributed the questions. I had the answers by heart, without reference.

James then withdrew, and while a ballot was taken another two candidates went through the same drill. He continued:

> Finally we were all three summoned in, told we had been elected members of the Faculty, congratulated by the Dean and then walked off in procession led by him to Court No. 8 where Lord Migdale read out the affirmation to each of us in turn, we repeating it in phrases after him, and then signing our names in the Roll. Lord M. then gave us a brief address and off we went to the voting-room for further congratulation and hand-shaking. The Dean then led us off to be introduced to Da (!) which was formally done, and we then returned, robed and wigged ourselves and sallied out again to meet Rupert Smith of Shepherd + Wedderburn, Macpherson and Mackay W.S., who gave me a divorce summons to draft – my first brief.

After having lunch with Jack Mackenzie Stuart (who had been his devil-master) at the Faculty restaurant, James worked on the summons and completed it that evening, giving him time to have dinner with his parents. 'A brass plate was put up by my bell at No. 5', he later noted in his diary, 'and the old family one on the inside door.' The latter bore the words: 'Mr. Clyde, Advocate.'

Chapter 3

Mr Clyde, Advocate

On 25 July 1959, the London *Evening Standard* reported that 'the third generation of a famous Scottish legal family has been admitted to the Faculty of Advocates in Edinburgh'. That third generation was, of course, James, who was now to work at Parliament House alongside his father. James's grandfather had died in 1944, although his widow Anna Margaret was still alive when her grandson was studying at Edinburgh University.[1]

By the late 1950s, James's father had been Lord President of the Court of Session for almost five years, during which he had established himself as a domineering presence. 'He was decisive and never wasted time on second thoughts,' recalled Sir David Edward decades later. 'His deceptively simple judgments dealt only with the essential points, stated the law tersely and clearly, and rarely provoked dissent.'

He was not, however, universally loved, for Hamish did not suffer fools gladly (legal or otherwise), possessed a deep

---

1   Anna Margaret was known for her prolific needlework, which included a large wall tapestry at Briglands and a bedspread later displayed by the National Trust of Scotland. It was said she did her work in the mornings, waiting for her husband to come down for breakfast. When James's sister Ann was a baby, she struggled to pronounce her grandmother's name so settled on 'Gaga', a name that stuck.

contempt for bureaucracy and took no trouble to hide it. He stubbornly rejected the requests of Scottish newspaper editors to install a photocopier in the press room, and would micro-manage – for good or ill – every aspect of life in the Faculty.

On being called to the Bar, James was prohibited from living with a judge (i.e. his father), thus his move to 5 Heriot Row, where he replaced a couple of eminent classical musicians. It was to remain his home until his marriage a few years later. It was not without problems, for the bathroom had a tendency to leak and the kitchen was 'very depressing'. With time he made some improvements, as well as developing the garden at the rear of the house, salvaging a length of balustrade from the façade of the original New Club building (demolished in the 1960s) in order to separate the stone flagging from the flower beds.

James also found himself surrounded, as he had been as a child, by fellow lawyers in what was known as the 'Square Mile', an area in which solicitors could distribute their papers with relative ease. Upstairs was a lecturer in Administrative Law at Edinburgh University, next door at No. 6 was Gordon Coutts (not yet a QC), and nearby were 'Tiger' Burns and Jack Macfie, the latter a senior partner at Tods Murray and 'popularly recognised as the best dressed solicitor in Edinburgh'. Douglas Reith and his family were in the top flat of No. 11, while Douglas Cullen (later Lord Cullen) inhabited the bottom apartment. Lionel Daiches, QC, also lived for a while in the first-floor flat of No. 10; the bottom flat at No. 8 was owned by Alastair Johnson, later Lord Dunpark; and Sheriff Archie Bell (and later Sheriff William Christie) resided at No. 1. Much later, Nigel (later Lord) Emslie would live at No. 2.

Emslie, like James, was the son of a judge, and they were by no means alone; indeed of the fifteen judges on the Court of Session bench at that time, five (including Hamish Clyde) had sons at the Bar. One Faculty wag even proposed setting aside a small room for those who were *not* sons of judges, so they could pass comment on members of the bench without fear or favour. The total occupancy of the Bar could be measured in tens (a total of 100–110) rather than, within a couple of decades, in hundreds, all of them practising from the elegant Advocates' Library.

Inevitably in such an intimate environment, James would appear before his father on a number of occasions, provoking mutterings to the effect that this was unfairly to his advantage. Hamish Clyde had had a similar experience appearing before his own father three decades before, but in James's case they were understandable yet unjustified: he was to carve out his career at the Bar as a result of unremitting hard work, a strong sense of justice and his own outstanding skill as an advocate.

On 4 September 1959, James made his first appearance in Court, before Lord Mackintosh in Glasgow. The case concerned a group of men who had entered a public house in Hamilton, where they had tied up the barman and stolen, as he noted carefully in his diary, '30 bottles of whisky, 18 half bottles, 4000 cigarettes, £50 [in] money and some other drink – a bottle of rum and 3 bottles of stout'. Inconsistencies in the prosecution case meant James was able to avoid a guilty verdict (one of the accused had a good alibi), although he made 'one bad bloomer' in his 'first cross-examination'. 'In general, the case shows the value of preparation,' James reflected in his diary later that day, 'my study of the . . . stock sheets and bar records was valuable'. Back in Edinburgh he found another brief awaiting his attention. 'I hope I have learnt something today,' he added in his diary, 'especially from my mistakes.' Other entries from that period are full of self-criticism about his performance before certain judges.

The following month he acted as junior to Lionel Daiches QC (his neighbour on Heriot Row) in a bank theft case, again in Glasgow. Daiches made 'a magnificent speech' during which a female juror fainted, and from James's point of view he did not believe more 'could have been made of the little material we had' to defend their client, who was found guilty. But gratifyingly for a relatively fresh junior, in his mammoth summing up speech to the jury, Lord Wheatley included 'a few kind words' about James's 'brief but fairly full' plea in mitigation for the accused.

These were pretty routine cases of the sort assigned to young advocates, but more high profile was the case of William Dowie Kidd, a 35-year-old tractor man on a farm in Crail who was put on trial for the murder of his wife and fourteen-year-old daughter at the High Court in Perth. There had been a nation-wide search for Kidd when the body of his daughter Christina had been found near Dunfermline on 5 July. Later the same day his wife, also called Christina, was found dead at the family home. It looked like a pretty hopeless case for James to help defend: Kidd had sat his dead daughter in the front seat of his car and even stopped to ask passers-by where he could buy petrol, meaning there were eighty-three witnesses for the prosecution (although many had assumed she was asleep).

James, acting as junior to Douglas Reith QC, lodged a special defence of insanity (which he conceded was 'rather optimistic' in his diary), with 'diminished responsibility' their 'second line of defence' if that failed. It did, and Lord Strachan sentenced Kidd to fifteen years' imprisonment, which in the circumstances his defence team judged 'not too bad'. The case also generated a degree of press coverage, with several newspapers getting James's name wrong, for example 'Mr Iain J. Clyde' (*Evening News*) and 'Mr I. J. Clyne' (*Evening Dispatch*); only the *Scotsman* got it right. Even worse, the *Daily Mail* printed a photograph of James wrongly captioned as 'Mr. Douglas Reith, Q.C.' and the comment: 'A man who behaves like this is as mad as a hatter' (Reith had used those words to describe Kidd). James thought it was probably 'actionable' and was teased about it at Parliament House the following day.

On 29 October 1959 James made his first appearance in the First Division of the Court of Session, one of two divisions of the Inner House dealing with civil matters, and two months later returned to criminal matters when he dealt with the case of nineteen-year-old William Harold Livingstone, who was standing trial at Glasgow High Court for the murder of a two-year-old girl. Defending him, he argued that Livingstone had been trying to silence a crying child but did not consider his blow a heavy one. 'He was genuinely fond of the child,' he told the jury. 'What happened was a very great and terrible shock to him.' James also drew attention to his client's challenging upbringing, alluding to 'surroundings in which the use of violence is regarded as normal and in which the exercise of restraint is seldom considered'.

James had also mentioned that the youth's father had been murdered, but without realising it had been a cause célèbre in its day, a link that reporters quickly discovered and published alongside their coverage of the shocking trial. Although James got a 'good press' in the evening papers ('but unfortunately my speech was less well-phrased than yesterday's'), his involvement also attracted what he irreverently called a letter 'from an anonymous admirer' in his scrapbook, an anonymous correspondent who said they were 'shocked and horrified' to read of James 'pleading leniency for a <u>man that murdered that dear little innocent child</u>. You are not fit to be in that position.' 'Have you any family?' asked the letter, before adding with disdain: 'Shame on you.'

Not all of James's early workload was so public, and by the early 1960s he had undertaken a wide range of cases and built a reputation as a shrewd and able junior counsel, undramatic but generally sound. Although modest and somewhat self-effacing, he nevertheless had an attractive courtroom manner, cutting a debonair figure with his fresh complexion and deploying the force of his genial personality. Well prepared, his arguments were also carefully presented, and he was quick to take a point in argument, or indeed discard one which was not finding favour.

But while work took him all over Scotland, usually to towns and cities like Perth, Aberdeen and Glasgow, there was still plenty of time for golf, walks, theatre and cinema, and parties with friends. A long-standing Robert Burns aficionado, James delivered the toast to the lassies at the 57th anniversary dinner of the Scottish Burns Club and also frequently acted as organist at Old St Paul's Church in Edinburgh's Old Town. Sandy Wilkinson, who used to holiday with the Clydes, remembers that if they were abroad then James 'would seek an opportunity for organ practice in one of the local churches'.

Music remained a major passion, and in October 1960 James even bought a grand piano. Kenny Cameron later recalled joining James and another friend in playing a Schumann piano trio 'with a certain degree of seriousness', but 'then breaking off to stand round the piano and hilariously sing Flanders and Swann songs'. Wilkinson recalled James speaking of 'forming small instrumental groups', his interest in the cello having remained with him since his schooldays.

James also continued to travel, particularly to classical sites, visiting Istanbul in the summer of 1960 ('a crowded, busy, confused, disorganised jumble of a city'), quite an adventurous place to go at that time, while the following March he joined the rather more conventional 'Swan's Hellenic Cruise' (as did Lord and Lady Strachan) to indulge his love of the classical world. On board the ss *Ankara*, an American vessel handed over to the Turks, James listened to a lecture on 'Greece Today' by Sir John Wolfenden (who had in the late 1950s recommended the decriminalisation of homosexuality) before visiting Dubrovnik, Athens, the sites of Delphi and Mista, and Crete, where he saw the Minoan drainage system, 'wash-down closets, baths and seemingly all modern conveniences'.

'A civilisation was revealed to me which, though I had already known of it, now for the first time came alive,' he wrote breathlessly in his diary, 'a civilisation comparing favourably with our own in many particulars, superior in some respects to the glories of Greece and Rome.' All in all, James visited seventeen ports in four different countries, travelling as cheaply as he could (it cost him 95 guineas, which he considered 'a bargain'), 'looking to the holiday, the change, the experience, and the new understanding and interest I have gained of ancient history'. 'I should have done this before I read Greats,' he added. 'It is impossible to understand Greek history without going to Greece; I return an ardent Phil-Hellenic, full of wonder and admiration, with a mind rich in memories.'

Back at Parliament House, Clyde was invited by James Mackay, later Lord Mackay of Clashfern, to assist him in revising a standard textbook on valuation for (local government) rating, *Armour on Valuation*, which had last been published in 1912. The law had been reformed in 1956 and the first revaluation under the new Rating (Scotland) Act was due to take place in 1961; when Mackay's original co-author failed to come up with the goods he turned to James in the knowledge that he could work quickly and diligently.

Together they breathed new life into a celebrated but half-century-old textbook, James demonstrating the easy literary style which was a hallmark of his later judicial work. Thus *Armour on Valuation for Rating* (third edition) by J. P. H. Mackay and J. J. Clyde appeared in time to meet great demand. Rating was a peculiarly recondite area of the law, but it was one in which both Clyde and Mackay would excel, later co-editing two further revisions of the book,[2] and James in particular becoming heavily involved in Rating case work along with a more general civil practice extending over reparation, administrative law, tax and trust work.

In August 1961, for example, James dealt with a Valuation Appeal Committee in Ayr and another in Edinburgh, with similar work taking up what remained of that year and the one

---

2　The fifth edition was co-edited by James and David Hope in 1985.

after. At a Rating Conference in October 1963 he presented a paper entitled 'Some Observations on Scottish Valuation Appeals' and even wrote a poem called 'The Assessor's Dream or A Night Mare', which rather betrayed how all-consuming the work had become.[3] He and James Mackay were also regulars at the Valuation Appeal Court, appearing before the Lords Sorn, Patrick and Hill-Watson. 'James and I could tell with precision what the court was likely to do which greatly enhanced our reputation with the appellants,' recalled Mackay, 'and we were always right.'

In 1961 James also made his debut on a breach of contract case in the House of Lords, the highest court of appeal for civil cases in Scotland and a portent of his later role as a Lord of Appeal in Ordinary, or Law Lord. He spent a week at Westminster during July, and reflected in his diary that his 'closer acquaintance' to the Appellate Committee (of the House of Lords) had 'not increased my admiration for them'. 'The first impression, on Monday, was purely of wonder and respect – for the swiftness of intellect and the clarity of reasoning. As the days passed the magic seemed to disappear and at the last while I would not presume to look for feet of clay I was at least disappointed.'

James also watched 'Mr. Wedgwood Benn' (otherwise known as Tony) arguing before the Election Appeal Court 'on the question of whether he is obliged to surrender his seat in the House of Commons now that he has succeeded to the peerage' (Benn's father, Viscount Stansgate, had died, thus barring him from a seat in the Lower House). 'He argued fluently,' noted James in his diary, 'but it seemed to me more with the skill of a politician than the ability of a lawyer.'

In January 1962, James celebrated his 30th birthday and was considering marriage. He had met Ann Hoblyn five years

---

3   Later, James would also compose some lines 'in contemplation of an icy January and a frozen valuation roll'.

earlier through mutual friends of his parents. Ann was finishing her midwifery training at the Western General Hospital in Edinburgh. Just like James's mother and grandmother, who were both English, Ann had a similar background. Her parents lived in Kent, she went to school at Sherborne and had trained as a Nightingale Nurse at St Thomas's Hospital in London. However, Ann was in fact half Scottish and had spent the war with her grandparents in Perth, and had frequently holidayed north of the border.

Following a dinner arranged by James's mother at Heriot Row, Ann had come to stay in Edinburgh in October 1957 (but went straight 'to bed with a cold', according to James's diary). Years later, just before he died, James told his nurses in hospital that he had fallen in love with Ann the first time they met.

The following autumn, the staff at Briglands were intrigued when a young woman arrived alone on her red scooter all the way from Perth. By 1959, a romance was kindling, but it would be several years before it caught fire: Ann had accepted a posting as a nursing sister with the Colonial Service in Hong Kong. She had been born in the Far East and was anxious to experience the region, and James did not want to interfere with her plans.

James, therefore, waited patiently for Ann to return, keeping in touch through regular letters. As it happened, she returned to the UK a year early having contracted a serious viral infection. In the summer of 1962, James drove down to Kent and on 8 August, he recorded in his diary, quite simply: 'Became engaged to Ann Hoblyn.' Later that day, James took his fiancée into the local town, Tunbridge Wells, to buy her an engagement ring. Muriel Hoblyn, his future mother-in-law, was shocked to hear where it had been purchased, exclaiming: 'That shop sells only stolen goods!'

A few days later, James's parents came down from Scotland to meet Ann's relatives, an important event as his father rarely left Scotland. 'Then Ma and Da and the Hoblyns talk,' he wrote in his diary, 'and a tiring, exhausting and emotionally trying day.'

But it is clear how happy he was. 'Bless Da and Ma,' he added, 'for being wonderful parents.' More of the extended Clyde clan arrived a few days later, with Ann's parents, Donald and Muriel Hoblyn, hosting a lunch at their home, Glenside.

They planned to get married at the end of that year but Ann's health meant the wedding was postponed until August 1963. They were finally married at St James's Church in Piccadilly at 11am on 10 August, with Kenny Cameron as best man. James's sister Ann and her family came over from Paris for the wedding. Ann's eldest daughter Caroline and Ann's cousin Tricia Hoblyn were bridesmaids. There was a reception at the United Services Club and then James and Ann took a flight to Geneva, where they were driven to the Cottage Hotel on Lake Annecy.

It was the beginning of what would become a happy and enduring family life with Ann, whom James called 'Sweetie'. James's uncle Bill DuBuisson had once said to Ann, 'I hope you realise you're marrying a Clyde,' as if that explained everything. Helpfully he then went on to elaborate: 'You just have to remember three things. Firstly, work is the most important thing. Secondly, Briglands will always come next. And thirdly, you!'

In James's case, he managed to give all three fairly equal attention, being a particularly supportive husband throughout Ann's recuperation. The earlier viral infection had damaged her liver, which delayed them starting a family for six years and which would weaken her for the rest of her life. He was also 'considerate and fun'; Ann recalled with affection the time they celebrated a wedding anniversary sitting on a rock in Sandwood Bay, a remote corner of Sutherland. When a solemn-looking German tourist suddenly appeared out of the mist, James offered him some champagne in a plastic cup. The bemused visitor left later with a great smile.

Since the year of his engagement, James had been involved in what was known as the Burmah Oil case, in which the company sought compensation for the destruction of its installations in Rangoon in 1942, on the orders of the British Government, to prevent their falling into the hands of the advancing Japanese forces. In February 1963, the case reached the First Division of the Court of Session, where James's father officiated as Lord President. James, who acted as junior counsel to Harry Keith QC on behalf of the pursuers (Burmah Oil), cited a 1920 House of Lords case, which held that necessity might justify the acquisition by the Crown of a subject's property, but necessity did not deny that subject the right to compensation.

James also argued that, unlike English Law, Scots Common Law had acquired from Roman and Continental authorities recognition of the idea that when the property of a private individual was destroyed in the public interest (and for the sake of peace) then compensation should be paid. Putting his classical education to good use, he quoted from the Code of Justinian published in AD 529, submitting that where there was an 'equitable principle' it ought to be possible to enforce it in the courts. When Lord Sorn pointed out that that was 'just the opposite of what has been laid down by English law', James replied: 'Happily we are on the other side of the Border.'

The Lord President, however, decided that Burmah Oil was not entitled to £60 million in compensation as their assets had been lawfully seized on the orders of the British Crown. In this instance, no one could have accused him of favouring his son in court. When, in early 1964, the company appealed the dismissal of their claims in the House of Lords, James was again present, and this time they were successful. Thereafter *The Times* lambasted the Government in an editorial, arguing (with good reason) that its threat to pass retrospective legislation to indemnify the Crown against Burmah Oil's claim amounted to interference with due legal process. The case continued to occupy James's time when, in December 1964, he was asked to advise on the constitutional position when the Government introduced a Bill to end the claim once and for all. This, he wrote in his diary, was 'intensely interesting'.

His role in the Burmah Oil case was an indication of James's growing standing at the Bar, where his work was full of stimulation and even entertainment. In May 1963, he had spent a morning in Glasgow inspecting the route taken by a trolley bus 'in which a man said he had fallen asleep and . . . then fell down a pit trying to make his way out'. He was even 'allowed to drive a trolley bus (on battery power) out of the shed and in by another door. Not difficult to steer and a sense of great power.' And in October 1964 he sat as Assessor in the Burgh Court in a complaint against a bookseller for supplying an apparently 'indecent' book called *Fanny Hill* to a police officer. 'Read it in the afternoon,' noted James in his diary. 'It is an abridged edition and not all that awful.'

As ever, he made time for extra-legal activities, both before and after his marriage to Ann, usually games of golf, visits to church or trips to the theatre with his parents. In May 1964, for example, James was present at a memorable dinner to mark the centenary of the Speculative Society, at which the Duke of Edinburgh and Prime Minister (Sir Alec Douglas-Home) were present ('An array of speakers, good food by candlelight and good entertainment'), while later that year he watched the Duke's wife, the Queen, open the Forth Road Bridge, although it 'could hardly be seen through the mist'. That evening he and Ann drove to Briglands via the new bridge for the first time. 'The toll is 2/6', James noted in his diary (he liked to record how much things cost), 'and you hand it to a man as you go past him almost without stopping.' Finally, 1964 was brought to a close with carol singing at Lord and Lady Grant's. 'Great fun,' thought James. 'Lord Kilbrandon at the piano and a large gathering.'

Just how busy (and happy) James was at this point in his life can be seen from his collection of papers. His court work was busier and higher profile than ever before (he took care to save pertinent newspaper cuttings), while in 1966 he was still typing up his old diaries from 1951. In April 1965, he was appointed Standing

Junior Counsel to the Forestry Commission in Scotland, and he was also regularly instructed (as was David Hope) as one of a select team of counsel by the National Coal Board, at that time a frequent litigator due to mining accidents.

He clearly venerated Scots Law, even considering an attempt to declare the Government's War Damages Act invalid 'on the grounds of it being unconstitutional and contrary to the Act of Union'. 'I felt quite sad at the injustice of it,' James wrote on 1 July 1965. 'This must be the most gross interference with the Courts that Scotland has seen for centuries, if ever,' a belief that reflected his deep interest in Scotland's history and distinct institutions. The following year, Scottish justice won plaudits abroad when the US arm of Gillette joined forces with its English-based firm to enforce its patent covering treated stainless-steel razor blades, having accused three Scottish firms of infringing its intellectual property.

In a trial lasting nearly a month, James was third junior (to QCs George Emslie and James Mackay) in the legal team acting on behalf of Gillette, positing a case full of scientific testimony praised by Lord Avonside as meticulous. The company magazine even carried pictures of James and the rest of the legal team, saying their victory 'constituted an impressive demonstration of the sound administration of justice in Scotland'. Philip Colman, patent counsel for Gillette in Boston, later wrote to thank James personally.

In September 1969, Ann gave birth to a son, James Donald Lawrence Clyde, or 'Jamie', whom James senior collected from hospital and filmed with a new cine camera he had purchased the previous week. 'He made little sounds, kicked, and then discovered that the thumb of his right hand would fit into his mouth,' he wrote in his diary that evening. 'Spent an hour telephoning relatives and friends. Had a meal at Hendersons and went to bed still half in dream.'

Two years later, James took Silk, becoming a QC like his father and grandfather before him. His friend and neighbour

John Macfie wrote to congratulate him on 3 August 1971. 'I remember meeting your Father one day at Stockbridge just after you had been announced as Dux of the Academy,' he recalled. 'I said to him, mindful of his and your Grandfather's record of being Dux of the Academy, that you only had one thing to do now! All my best wishes to that pinnacle.'

Chapter 4

What a Strange Thing Politics Is!

The 1970s were a turbulent decade politically and economically, and for James it brought both highs — taking Silk, promotion as an advocate depute and another son — and lows — frustrated ambitions both at the Faculty of Advocates and in the political realm. Having progressed steadily and satisfactorily since leaving school twenty years earlier, for the first time he began to feel the burden of expectation. 'My birthday. I am 40,' James wrote in his diary on 29 January 1972. 'When life begins so they say but I am not yet aware of it.'

Indeed, the era of the second Lord Clyde, James's father Hamish, had drawn to a close a few weeks later when he stood down as Lord President following almost two decades at the helm. He retired from the bench confident Scotland's legal system was the best in the world, and in late March the First Division courtroom was packed with a full contingent of fourteen judges, members of the Faculty, court staff and members of the public for a short farewell ceremony. Poignantly, by 'a singular stroke of providence', the last counsel to appear before the outgoing Lord President earlier that day had been James. Norman Wylie, the Lord Advocate, paid Hamish a humorous but warm tribute, to which (in James's account) he 'made a very fine reply'.

It is clear from James's diary that he had mixed feelings about his father's retirement. 'Parliament House will not be the same without Da around', he reflected, 'and yet in some way it will be some comfort not to have the mark of a reflected glory and the awkwardness of reticence and lack of criticism which has sometimes featured in conversation on the part of members of the faculty who perhaps feel that what is said to me may be said to Da.' He had always been conscious that the Clyde name could be both a blessing and a curse.

The new Lord President was the moustachioed George Emslie, who was patrician but invariably courteous with counsel, in contrast to his notoriously peremptory predecessor. James considered him 'a great lawyer', but also 'a more dignified and solemn figure'. 'The majesty and respect of the law will be upheld,' he predicted, 'but the humanity will not be so evident.'

Emslie's son Nigel was called to the Scottish Bar at around this time, having earlier devilled for James for around three months. He recalled visiting his devil master at Heriot Row to find Jamie Clyde playing, and the almost-ritual serving of tea and cake (after court), usually to make up for the lack of a proper lunch. Emslie added:

> James was always very good to me, and very good as a devil master. The first time we were instructed to do an opinion it came with 17 questions and all seemed very complicated. He came along and said 'how are you getting along?' and, seeing that I was having difficulty, said 'right, let's get something on paper, and see what it looks like'. Suddenly, in an hour we had something to work with and it was just a case of fleshing it out, not wasting time with nebulous research. He was always full of bonhomie and generous with his time.

James's father, meanwhile, prepared to vacate Heriot Row after four decades, and reside permanently at Briglands, designed

for his father, the first Lord Clyde, by the architect Sir Robert
Lorimer. There he would tend to his garden, model railway
and extensive library, 'happiest in old clothes, with a pipe in his
mouth and his much-loved wife at his side'. Remembering his
father's friends and contemporaries, figures from his childhood,
James observed in his diary that it was 'sad in a way how the
wheel turns'.

During 1972, the wheel also continued to turn for James.
His appointment as Silk the previous year had meant withdraw-
ing as counsel to both the Forestry Commission in Scotland
and Edinburgh Corporation, but for the first time he became
the grandly named Chancellor to the (Episcopalian) Diocese of
Argyll (his father had fulfilled the same honour for the Bishop of
Moray), as well as a member of the Scottish Valuation Advisory
Committee, an obvious appointment given his expertise in the
complex realm of local government rating.

And, for the first time, politics also beckoned as a possible
career (James had become an 'approved' Conservative candidate
that July), although one he saw largely in terms of increasing
his chances of becoming Lord Advocate and therefore fulfill-
ing the next stage of the traditional Clyde CV. As 1972 ended,
the current incumbent, Norman Wylie QC, invited him to the
Crown Office to meet the intimidatingly titled Squadron Leader
Ronald Kinsley-Brown, Wylie's election agent in Edinburgh
Pentlands (Norman was also a Member of Parliament, as
was usually the case at that time). James recounted the scene
thus:

> They propose to advance me as candidate for the
> Pentlands. Wylie is to retire and not stand again at the
> next general election. What a prospect before me. I
> have been contemplating a constituency but evidently
> lack of experience tells against me. North Edinburgh
> had been particularly attractive but the other day they
> decided upon some man from Cramond. Wylie says

they don't like lawyers and I hope that was why they
didn't even put me on a short list. Obviously, he has
been pushing me forward behind the scenes. I should
have so much to thank him for if the prospects in
Pentlands materialises, but they are still very remote.
I have yet to be selected far less elected. But it is good
to have something to work for. I must now start to get
my name known there. They say write to the papers.
They say take an active part in party work. So, I shall
have to do my bit.

It was certainly an incredible opportunity for James, the offer
of a safe Conservative seat (then becoming scarcer in a Scottish
context) and thereafter the Crown Office should Edward Heath
(the Prime Minister) continue in office after the next election.
But, as ever, there was a note of self-doubt. 'It seems to me every
chance is offered,' he added in his account of the meeting, 'and
I should be myself at fault if I fail.'

James was being unduly harsh on himself, although subsequent events justified his caution. A few days later he was in
a reflective mood as 1972 gave way to a new year, and the
UK's membership of the Common Market (later the European
Union) on 1 January 1973 which, as he observed perceptively,
'most respect because they do not understand and few guess
what it may involve'. He continued:

> For us a year of a few outstanding moments but a
> forward-looking year with the prospect of a new baby
> in July and a possible entry in the public life and pol-
> itics for me. It is good to look forward and it is better
> to look forward to a positive . . . goal. I have so long
> gone on working for a vague future, or often with my
> head so far down that I could not see where I was
> going or what I was going to. Now there is something
> to aim for, even although it is a mirage or even if the

future turns out so differently than it may now appear. However, we shall see.

The following year, James threw himself into political activity, diligently following Norman Wylie's advice. He helped canvass voters in Central Edinburgh, spoke at public meetings, mingled with office-bearers in the Edinburgh Pentlands Conservative Association and attended the annual Scottish Tory conference in Perth, where he made a contribution to the debate on law and order ('I said nothing very great,' he wrote in his diary, 'and see now what I could have said'). Although he was not a natural political animal, this was all part of his attempt 'to acquire experience and involvement in the party and try and have something of a history'.

On 13 July 1973 James was woken at 3am by a telephone call telling him he had another son, who would be called Timothy. 'Hooray. Hooray,' he wrote later. 'I got up, dressed and drove down to see Sweetie and the baby – rather crumpled and looking like granny. Very sweet. So thankful all is over and well over.' He then went on to Parliament House, 'with barely any sleep', and somehow kept himself conscious to attend a black-tie function in the evening honouring Margaret Kidd's fifty years at the Scottish Bar.[1]

Later that summer James called on the Lord Advocate, who told him his decision not to contest the next general election would be made in early November. Wylie also offered him a post as an advocate depute, which he accepted, although he was clearly in two minds. 'Felt considerably upset at this as it upsets

---

1   Coincidentally, Kidd, the first woman called to the Scottish Bar, had started her legal training with Ann's mother, Muriel Hoblyn (then Little), although Muriel gave up her training early after her sister Clunie died of rheumatic fever, returning to the family home in Perth to support her parents. Ann's father, John Little, was also in law, a solicitor and senior partner at J. & J. Miller in Perth.

the even tenor of my ways,' he wrote on 31 August, 'but that is ridiculous when I am deliberately planning to upset them if politics will have me. But I remained discouraged and apprehensive. The job will show me the Crown Office which will be a good thing but how settled and easy in one's ways one can become.'

The new post took effect on 1 October, and represented something of a gear-shift in career terms, with James moving from a large and successful civil practice to prosecuting criminal cases on behalf of the Crown at the High Court in Edinburgh. The political wheels, meanwhile, continued to turn. On 15 November, he was invited formally to put himself forward for the Pentlands nomination. Of course he did so – 'I do so much want not to miss this opportunity' – but a week later the Association informed him rather abruptly that he would not even be interviewed, a snub to both him and Norman Wylie, who had done so much to promote him as his successor. Ultimately, they opted for another advocate, an articulate young Edinburgh councillor called Malcolm Rifkind.

Naturally, James was gloomy. 'Oh dear, oh dear,' he wrote in his diary. 'This seems an awful let down   after the good introduction too. And having set my course on one track I seem now to be on the wrong line altogether. But I still hope against hope.' It was typical of him to maintain a brave face in disappointing circumstances, but, in reality, finding a similarly safe seat would be difficult. Still, James did his best, asking the local Conservative Party 'to be considered for any constituency'.

Eventually he was adopted as the Conservative candidate for Dundee East in a snap general election called by Edward Heath on 28 February 1974, amid a global oil crisis and industrial action, a context which rather set the tone for the remainder of that decade. The constituency ranged from the mainly middle-class suburb of Broughty Ferry to sprawling post-war council housing estates. The discovery of North Sea oil had transformed Dundee harbour, and James was careful to contrast his desire for that new commodity to benefit everyone in the

UK with the Scottish National Party's narrow and parochial slogan, 'It's Scotland's Oil'.

The SNP was strong in Dundee, with Gordon Wilson (a future leader of the party) having come close to winning a recent by-election. James told the *Dundee Courier* that most Scots did not want independence, but rather 'a degree of devolution which will enable the voice of Scotland to be more plainly heard in the government of Scottish affairs'. This was not, strictly speaking, the official Conservative Party line, but he said several times that his focus (if elected) would be the proposed Scottish Assembly and legislation for handling juvenile crime.

But while party workers distributed stickers proclaiming, 'I'm on Clyde's Side!', Dundee East was never, in reality, a realistic prospect as a Tory constituency. The electoral landscape of Scotland had changed significantly since the days of James's father and grandfather, both of whom had represented Edinburgh seats in Parliament. Not only was the Conservative Party in decline, but Scottish Nationalism was on the rise. Still, James gave it his all, and in late February Sarah Mudie, a supporter from Broughty Ferry (where Tory support was largely concentrated), wrote to wish him luck: 'You've certainly made an impact, which is wonderful, considering the minimal time you've had to do so.'

On 28 February, James toured polling stations in the constituency with Ann, and at 11pm made his way to the 'count' at Dundee's City Hall. 'Mildly nervous,' he admitted in his diary, 'and depressing as I saw too few bundles of my vote and too many of the others.' Gordon Wilson, the SNP candidate (also a lawyer), came first, Labour second and James third with a respectable 13,371 votes. 'A change from Labour at least,' he wrote in his diary, 'but a depressing swing to the SNP. Gloomy news of the election results from all over.' James's election agent had said to him after the count: 'I'm afraid you are too honest for this job!'

It was at least a consolation to James that even had he been elected, there would have been no immediate prospect of becoming Lord Advocate. given the formation of a minority Labour government with Harold Wilson once again Prime Minister. Still, he had managed to increase the Conservative share of the vote vis-à-vis the March 1973 by-election and the local association seemed content, later telling him that it had not 'had a previous Candidate who commanded our respect and wholehearted support as you have done'. Given that neither Labour nor the Conservatives had an overall majority, another general election was not impossible, and so on 8 March James asked the Scottish Tory grandee Sir William Younger for advice. 'Dundee wants me back and I am not too anxious to go,' he noted in his diary. 'He [Sir William] said not to hurry.'

On 22 March, James watched the new Lord Advocate, Ronald King Murray QC, being sworn in before calling on him to resign as an advocate depute, which given the change of government he was expecting. He then resumed his former civil practice, and as if the disappointment of the election was not enough, just over a week later James's mother died following a short illness. The funeral took place on 4 April, but her husband, James's father, was too ill to attend. 'So many memories of her love and care over so many years, of life at 14 Heriot Row, of picnics and journeys and holidays,' he wrote in his diary. 'She must have been a saint. So much courage and such determination.' A memorial service took place at St Mary's Cathedral at the end of May.

It was an unhappy period, not least because James now had to organise the care for his father at Briglands, where he spent more and more time. In May 1974, he was appointed a chairman of Medical Appeal Tribunals in Scotland, while throughout most of that summer and autumn he and his colleague David Hope drove up and down to the picturesque north-west village of Drumbuie, the locus of a long-running controversy and public inquiry concerning proposals to build ten oil platforms.

The inquiry had begun the previous year with a degree of confusion. Having been led by a junior's briefing to believe his clients were in favour of the development, James began their first meeting in pre-emptory fashion. 'Well, gentlemen,' he declared: 'We're in favour of this development.' After an awkward pause, the leader of the delegation said, 'no, we're against it,' on environmental and aesthetic grounds, and without batting an eyelid James immediately proceeded to give a masterly examination of all the objections which ought to be raised, reorientating so skilfully that the clients did not properly grasp that anything was amiss.

James came to enjoy the trips north every other weekend in a Volkswagen hired by Hope, driving up on a Sunday, often in terrible weather, and then returning south the following Friday, usually in challenging gales. 'Back in the same hotel, same room, same inquiry,' he wrote wistfully on 10 March 1974. 'But I feel more cheerful about it this time. So much has happened since this inquiry started. Here I was at the start thinking I might be candidate in the Pentlands. Now here I am having fought an election in Dundee. All so unexpected.'

That September, as Jamie started school at Denham Green (the junior department of the Edinburgh Academy Preparatory School), the Government rejected the proposal on environmental grounds, even though the deep-water site in Drumbuie was considered one of the most suitable in the UK for constructing the huge concrete oil rigs required by the booming energy sector. Oil, meanwhile, continued to loom large politically as preparations for another general election got under way. James still harboured ambitions to enter Parliament, but his overtures to the local Conservative Associations in West Perthshire (where Nicholas Fairbairn was being considered) and West Edinburgh were both rebuffed. 'Very depressed,' he wrote in his diary. 'Seems that nothing goes right.'

Still he held out hope that an opportunity would arise, and indeed in August he was sounded out about becoming the candidate in West Perthshire after all, chiefly because it seemed Fairbairn was not to everyone's taste. James went to see a local Tory official called Scott-Davidson to discuss the situation further. 'He wants to have someone up his sleeve to counter the defence that no alternative could be found in time,' he wrote in his diary. 'I agreed that if the constituency was looking for a candidate and did not have one I was interested. What a strange thing politics is!' Strange indeed, but in the event Fairbairn survived, something that so infuriated James's father (who lived in the constituency) that he cast his (postal) vote for the Scottish Nationalist candidate, even though Fairbairn had served as his ADC during his own election campaigns in North Edinburgh in the early 1950s.

James did not much like the idea of the flamboyant Fairbairn being an MP (or indeed Lord Advocate) either, although he realised the prospect of a Conservative victory was remote. On 10–11 October 1974, he stayed up with Ann until 3am watching the election results come in, but by the morning it was clear Labour had a small overall majority. 'So, I am glad I am not there after all,' he wrote in his diary. 'Fairbairn won Kinross with a miserable majority of 53 after two recounts. A disgrace from a former majority of over 8000! But the Scottish Nationalists have made enormous headway.' Indeed, having won seven MPs that February, the SNP now emerged from the election with eleven.

Just after Christmas, James reflected on another busy year, observing that he was more tired than usual and that he longed 'to get things tidier and get the garden into shape'. His father, who needed more help at Briglands, also occupied his mind, and indeed a few days later suffered another stroke. At home in Edinburgh James and Ann had help two or three afternoons a week from the 'faithful elderly Mrs Canning', known by Jamie as 'Nana', but James was finding his two sons 'a bit of a handful, especially as Timothy is beginning to find his feet'. In April 1975, James and Ann holidayed in Italy, including a visit to the

Vatican in Rome, and then at the end of June Hamish died at Briglands aged seventy-six.

Although his father's death was not unexpected, it still came as a shock to James, especially coming just a year after that of his mother. He wrote a lengthy appreciation for the *Scotsman*, which referred to his father's 'hard work coupled with a thorough grasp of legal principles and a capacity for skilful presentation of a case' and observing – perhaps with his own recent experience in mind – that he had not found 'the rough and tumble of the House of Commons to his taste'. It continued:

> For Scots Law and the traditions of the law, he had a deep respect and affection, and resisted valiantly what he regarded as any encroachment on its scope, from whatever quarter it came. His opinions were strongly held and vigorously expressed – the vigour tempered by a sometimes-youthful humour. It was one of his great charms that in many respects he never lost the zest of youth: even his continuing and boyish inter-ests in trains and railways, and his enjoyment of simple things. His love of Scotland and things Scottish was a very real thing; a part of his being; and he was never happier than when he could throw off the cares of his office and return to his country home; to his garden and to the surrounding hills. A certain personal shy-ness never left him; but, among his colleagues and his friends, he showed the essential kindliness and simplic-ity of his character.

It would be for others, concluded James, to evaluate his father's qualities as a judge, 'but for one, who for over 60 years enjoyed the privilege of his staunch friendship in good days and bad, the world and Scotland will be an emptier place without Hamish Clyde'. It was a moving tribute from a son to his father.

In July, James fell ill and had to have an operation, meaning he 'staggered' to his father's memorial service at St Mary's Cathedral. By September he was still feeling melancholy, writing in his diary how different everything seemed, even his work, 'as if the old life has ended. Perhaps it is still something of the shock of death.' Further rejections from the Leith and Edinburgh South Conservative Associations did not help, although he felt relief as well as disappointment.

In November 1975 James's 'Uncle Dick', to whom he had been close, also died in the south of England. In his diary, James observed that Richard and his father had never really been close, 'each going their own way', but he had fond memories of his uncle 'as a jolly and friendly person, a great host in London to a little boy from Edinburgh. He seemed the cosmopolitan to the provincial.' At Hogmanay, James was praying that the new year would 'be a better one than this'.

'The past, present and future seem to be close when one clears out papers,' mused James to his diary on 8 January 1976. 'And the future of the Court of Session does not seem certain. Certainly, the amount of good litigation is diminishing and people are wondering what is going to happen. Judicial appointment seems remote. Time goes on and I seem to get nowhere. It is hard to be confident.'

Nevertheless, in late 1975 and throughout 1976, James kept up his political activity, planning a candidacy in the new Scottish Assembly which he and many others assumed would soon be established in Edinburgh, taking part in a debate on the new Radio Forth commercial station, conducting the case for pubs opening on Sundays in a mock trial – the 'jury' backed him 13–2 in favour ('it was all great fun'). But what dominated that year was the sale of both Briglands ('one has to be practical in these days of economic difficulty') and the flat at No. 5 Heriot Row.

James and Ann had looked at No. 9, just a few doors along, which had once been the offices of Mackenzie & Black WS, although it had lain empty for several years and was thus in a rather sorry state. On 10 March, they got the keys again and found it 'so pleasant, appalling as its condition is, that we desperately wildly and hopelessly want it'. Indeed, so desperate that James even paid a little bit more than the asking price in a private transaction, assured by his surveyor that the market would more than compensate within six months. Another attraction was that it could be a home for some of furniture from Briglands.

It was to become the Clydes' family home for the next twenty years, a busy house always full of friends and family, and usually with tenants in the basement and student lodgers in the attic, while the car park to the rear proved an advantage as parking became more difficult on Heriot Row. By that autumn, just after Jamie had started at the Academy Prep School on Arboretum Road, James and Ann were busy packing up nearly twenty years of possessions to move four doors down the road from No. 5. 'Tea boxes in lots of places,' recorded James in his diary on 1 October, 'and piles and bags of bits.'

> Pictures came down, carpets come up and an era passes away. I remember sitting by the window on the floor of my library seventeen (is it!) years ago and contemplating the empty room into which I was going to move. Here I am now sitting at my desk, the room almost emptied again, with little Timothy dotting around taking paper out of the waste paper basket . . . The new house promises well despite its present chaos. Pray that we may all be as happy as we have been here.

Selling Briglands, however, proved trickier. The house was full of beautiful furniture, tapestries and a library accumulated by James's grandparents, all of which was catalogued by James. His sister Ann inherited much of the contents while James took over the house and the rest of the Briglands estate. But when it was put on the market, there proved little demand because it was too big for a private house and too small (with a difficult internal layout) to become a hotel or nursing home.

On top of the emotional wrench (it had been in the family for more than half a century), an issue was raised as one prospective buyer threatened to pull out when his wife became convinced the house was haunted. Interestingly, James (a rational lawyer, after all) did not dismiss this out of hand, as he well remembered his grandparents (and several others, usually female) talking of ghosts they associated, perhaps not entirely seriously, with the older wing of the house. Over the years, guests had commented on feeling a shivering feeling in one corridor on the first floor.

It was thought that, in Victorian times, a servant might have become pregnant and committed suicide by jumping out of the window on that corridor, and then had not been buried in consecrated ground. Having failed to substantiate this at Register House, James and Ann asked Bishop (Richard) Wimbush, a family friend, to hold a special Eucharist to dispel any haunting. He sprinkled holy water, gave communion and conducted special prayers. 'It was a powerful experience with a brilliantly conducted service,' James reflected in his diary. 'A strange day in every way.'

This appeared to resolve the haunting, for by the end of August, Briglands was being divided up for the benefit of three different purchasers. James found himself full of memories connected with 'that dear old house', but at the same time 'no great regret'. He wrote:

> I remember as a boy sitting in the Schoolroom and watching Gaga [his grandmother] in black walk across the lawn to the garden, to visit Wright the head gardener, a morning ritual. Further back there are memories of Mary Stewart, a buxom cook, dominating a busy kitchen with enormous energy. And a maid or two, uniformed in black with white aprons, who would open curtains in the morning. The war changed

the old order. Mrs Mitchell took over the housework. A kind hearted enormous woman who thought that she should never be discovered in her domestic duty and would disappear with tremendous clattering if anyone came along the passage near her – revealing her presence by sound more surely than the sight of her would ever have done . . .

It was not so long ago when Sweetie and I would go out there for a weekend from No. 5 with the parents and have meals cooked by the housekeeper and our beds turned down by her strange friend 'Dotty' Dorothy. But they passed on and the final stage was the odd Austrian couple who left when Da retired, leaving the parents to manage alone with only the daily help of Mrs. Milne from the village. So, the changing times and the decrease of staff have led to the greater difficulties of living in the place. I should have hated to see it decay about me and to see it as a weekend retreat from Edinburgh where home must be would be absurd.

It is odd how the house has changed as time has passed. This is perhaps why the parting now is not so bitter. It is not the place it was in Grandada or Gaga's day. Neither inside nor outside, in the gardens, is the maintenance anything like the grand day of the past. It has even changed since the parents were there. Changed even since those sad months of dear Da's decline, so that it is not the separation from something familiar and close, but only the leaving of a back cloth from which the forward scenery and the players have departed.

It was not, however, a complete break, for James arranged to keep the farm at Briglands and part of its garden, his plan being to construct a more modest home for him and Ann in the woods (they purchased a caravan at Rumbling Bridge as an interim residence).

The idea of creating a new house in the woods around Briglands came from Giovanna Kirby (known as 'GB'), a tourist from California who had turned up on the doorstep one evening on a bicycle. She had been touring Scotland, her bike had broken down and she needed a place to stay until she could get it repaired. She immediately hit it off with James and Ann and ended up staying for around a year, helping to look after the house in the period after Hamish's death and before it was sold. She catalogued the library at Briglands and collated family recipes. Her bicycle was never repaired.

Early one morning, James went for a walk around the estate and returned saying: 'I've found the spot for it.' At the western end of Briglands was a plantation of Christmas trees that had not been leased to the farmer who looked after the fields. In the middle of the plantation was an area of grass he thought was the perfect place for a house. As this area was cleared, it revealed a beautiful west-facing view stretching many miles down the valley to Stirling. This was a bonus, especially as the old house had no view at all.

A recognised modern architect called Michael Calthrop was brought on board. His initial advice was to move away from a wooden structure; the damp and wind of Scotland would not be compatible with a Scandinavian concept. So, a new design was drawn up and James created his own architectural model of the proposed house, thereafter working collaboratively with Michael. The result was a 1970s timber-frame design clad with brick-and-heather tiles and an unusually shaped roof. Calthrop retained the original log-cabin concept by incorporating wooden shutters. The design won an award.

The new house was called 'Shiel', also the name of the hill it stood on. During the initial construction, the Clydes would come out from Edinburgh to review progress, staying in their temporary caravan. Once the house was finished in 1980, work started on creating what was to become a large woodland garden. Before the big house had been sold, James and

Ann had moved a collection of azaleas up from its garden, the Victorian summer house (a wedding present to James's grandfather) and a sundial created by Sir Robert Lorimer from a farm roller.

Two gardening students from Edinburgh's Royal Botanic Garden were recruited, providing muscle and horticultural expertise as the plantation of larch and conifers was slowly replaced by lawns, beds of shrubs, a walled garden, a ha-ha and a Japanese garden. Shiel became the Clydes' pet project. For James, the process of creating the new house, and particularly its garden, was an important part of his later life, providing him with relaxation from the many stresses of his career, as well as a focus for his family.

The wider Briglands estate went through a slow transformation under James's stewardship. When he inherited it, Briglands had suffered from decades of post-war decline in investment. He slowly redeveloped the properties on the estate and diversified the income streams so that by the time of his death Briglands was in good fettle. James took over the caravan park adjoining the estate, which became a low-cost holiday retreat for generations of families. He also agreed to create a public footpath along the riverbank, which is now hugely enjoyed by the local community.

In 1991, the upstairs of Shiel was redeveloped and a glass solarium designed by local architect Fred Whalley added (Michael Calthrop had since moved to France). This became perhaps the most-enjoyed part of the house, with its wrap-around views of the garden and valley. Later, James added a 'Millennium Dome' folly (constructed from iron pillars of the former cattle steading from the farm that had burnt down) and a maze. All of this meant the 'new' Briglands became a much-loved haven for James and his family.

Just as all of this began to come together, in 1977, James found himself dwelling on his career, feeling a degree of frustration in his forty-fifth year that he had not achieved as much as he had anticipated in his twenties and thirties. He remained busy as a chairman of the Medical Appeal Tribunals in Scotland, while also following in his father's and grandfather's footsteps as a trustee of the National Library of Scotland. He stood down only in 1994.

In January 1977, the vice-deanship of the Faculty had fallen vacant, but after discussing his position with his colleague David Hope and James Mackay (the current Dean), James decided not to stand, although Mackay told him that Donald Ross, his predecessor as Dean, had viewed James as a successor ('an encouraging opinion'). 'David Hope assured me that not to be Vice-Dean did not mean not to be Dean next time,' James noted in his diary. 'So I begin to hope that I may in due course succeed James [Mackay] as Dean. They each said it was better not to stand than to stand and lose.'

Once again, he had in mind his father and grandfather, both of whom had led the Faculty. Later that year James was pressed to stand as Treasurer of the Faculty and understood that the Dean was keen that he should, 'but I do not want to, partly because it's not my cup of tea and partly because I don't want to get landed in a corner where I cannot readily stand as Dean'.

It was a difficult call and demonstrated how intensely political, at least for some, Parliament House could be, while in parliamentary terms James found himself torn between Westminster (as a route to the Crown Office) and the proposed new Scottish Assembly, which would be put to voters in a referendum in early 1979. He made the short list for the Conservative candidacy in Berwick and East Lothian at the end of 1977 but confessed to his diary that he was 'getting used to a quiet and comfortable life at home and don't want to be jolted out of it'. On the other hand, he was conscious that he might regret just drifting on 'without something more adventurous to show for my life'.

He clearly felt the shifting context of the late 1970s, recording at length in his diary the sight of some youths at King's

Cross station 'in the latest "punk rock" fashion of torn clothing ornamented with chains and safety pins and zips, either closed or open, cut hair partly coloured in wild purples and greens'. It also appealed to his sense of the absurd that this contrasted so sharply with 'a couple of elderly passengers obviously home from a fishing spell in the North with the bearing of an ex-army officer'.

James hoped 1978 would see his affairs 'more settled', both in respect of Briglands and his 'own ambitions'. Within a few months that was truer of the former – he settled Briglands Trust for the benefit of the next generation[2] – than the latter, although he clearly enjoyed the respect and affection of his peers. In September David Hope, an admirer since their Academy days and until recently James's junior, wrote to say what a privilege it had been working with him. 'On so many occasions it has been not merely an education but a delight to listen to your presentations, advanced with such skill, charm and good humour as few can hope to achieve,' he wrote from his home on India Street. 'The example is one which I value, but I shall find it hard to live up to it.'

Earlier that year, as Diocesan Chancellor, James had attended the enthronement of the Right Reverend George Kennedy Buchanan Henderson as Bishop of Argyll and the Isles on the Isle of Cumbrae, and was present, on 26 September 1978, when Prince Charles was made an honorary member of the Faculty of Advocates. As he recorded in his diary:

> I was introduced to him. He has a firm handshake and a modest manner, disdaining public honour as not due until he was grey haired and had achieved something but glad to be made an honorary member of Faculty in his

---

2   The Briglands estate (the farm and land remaining after the house was sold) was already in a trust established by James's father. In 1978, James varied the trust so that it could pass to his sons Jamie and Tim.

own right. He was refused the Freedom of Edinburgh some months ago and the connection between that and this honour was not unnoticed. It is something to have met the heir to the throne. I hope I shall do so again.

The following week, James was approached by Lord President Emslie (during a meeting of National Library trustees) about his willingness to serve as Lord Advocate were the Conservatives to be returned to office at the next general election. 'In other words several people realise that Nicholas Fairbairn (MP for Kinross) is not the man,' he wrote in his diary.

So the suggestion was that it should be me and if I had no constituency I should go to the Lords! Would I agree? I said of course I could and thanked the L.P. for agreeing on my behalf. He said he would continue to propose it when occasion occurred. So I returned home walking on air.

Chapter 5

A European Legal Profession

Becoming Lord Advocate would have represented the next step on a well-trodden Clyde path: James's grandfather, James Avon Clyde, had served as Scotland's most senior law officer between 1916 and 1920, while his son Hamish, James's father, had been at the Crown Office thirty years after that. Not only was it a coveted position, but its holder had the alluring option of appointing himself (and it had always been 'him' rather than 'her') Lord President.

But, as in his father's and grandfather's day, becoming one of two law officers (the other being Solicitor General for Scotland) normally required either a seat in the House of Commons or membership of the House of Lords. This explains why James spent much of the 1970s trying to cultivate Westminster constituencies and, that having failed, the same for anticipated (wrongly, as it turned out) elections to a devolved Scottish Assembly, and the European Parliament, which was to be directly elected for the first time in June 1979.

After being interviewed for a place on the Conservative candidates' list at the party's Central Office in London, James flew to Brussels on 20 October 1978 for a meeting of the Consultative des Barreaux de la Communauté Européenne (which later became the Council of the Bars and Law Societies of Europe) or CCBE, essentially a liaison committee for the legal profession across what later became the European Union, and an organisation that was to occupy a lot of his time over the next few years. James had been appointed by the Dean of the Faculty to represent the Scottish Bar.

Founded in 1960, the CCBE had ten full members (and others represented by observer delegations), but as the UK had only joined the European club at the beginning of 1973, Scots Law had only recently appeared on its radar. The UK and every other member state would appoint delegates to attend plenary sessions held two or three times a year in different towns by rotation. The aim was to study questions concerning the Bars and Law Societies of each member state against the backdrop of the Treaty of Rome, while co-ordinating the professional conduct of lawyers in each country, arguably a rather ambitious agenda.

James had first attended the CCBE in Bordeaux that April, shortly after its presidency had gone to his friend and colleague David Edward, whom he considered 'a patient but firm chairman' of a problematic organisation. 'Partly because the number is too large – between 20 and 30,' he elaborated in his diary. 'Partly because some members talk too much.' Proceedings were usually convivial but generally conducted in French, a language James found challenging, although he remained idealistic about creating 'a European legal profession'. In his diary, he wrote of

> great fraternity, a consciousness of many points of difference, a realisation of a great new unity in Europe, not in the immediate future but in the remote future in its final detail . . . an interest in other systems and in the points of difference that exist. It may be an exercise in international relations. In so far as person meeting person it achieves that. In building a European Bar, that is a long job. But it may be laying a foundation. There are problems in the status of the delegates – are they performing a European initiative or are they representing national views? Anyway, it has been interesting and

enjoyable. And I now return to the parish pump a little
more aware of the great world outside.

Back at the 'parish pump' he found himself approved as a prospective candidate for the European Parliament but everything,
as he wrote on 8 December 1978, was 'happening in the wrong
order'.

> I would like a general election first, so that I could
> know if the Crown Office is going to be left open
> for me. Or the Assembly – but that depends on the
> referendum which will not occur till March. And by
> then the European candidates must be chosen. It is all
> very puzzling. My preference is for the Crown Office
> or the Assembly and Europe comes last. But . . . it is
> going to occur first, as it looks at present. If only the
> government would fall!

It would soon fall, but there was a further complication when it
was announced that the salary for UK Members of the European
Parliament would be the same as that of a Westminster MP, just
under £7,000, which, even with additional allowances, made it
impossible for James to contemplate. 'Our scale of living is not
luxurious, but the necessary commitments of the house and the
boys' education makes Europe an impossible sacrifice,' he told
his diary. 'So, I have written to say I cannot apply for any seat
this time. It is disappointing, but yet in a way a relief.'

The winter of 1978 was one of the worst in living memory.
Briglands was snowed up and James and Ann could not even
get out of Edinburgh as 'the men who usually clear the snow
are on strike'. This was, of course, the Winter of Discontent,
which James must have hoped would bring down the Labour
government of James Callaghan and produce, as he wrote in
his diary, 'some certainty in the future'. At the end of January,
he was pleased when 'Old Lady Kinross (always indiscreet)'

asked: 'haven't you been appointed to the House of Lords or something?'

> I kept a poker face and pretended I didn't know what she meant, but her husband must have mentioned the plan whereby I might be there as a Crown Officer. I was cheered by this sign of the thinking. At present we are in a fearful state of industrial unrest – successive serious strikes and exorbitant pay claims. The government must face an election this year and at present their performance is not impressive. So, I wait for a change of government and the possible prospects there and for the Scottish Assembly – and also for an election for the Deanship of the Bar as I suspect James Mackay will go on the bench before many months have passed.

By February, industrial action had extended to civil servants, and even the courts stopped functioning. Then in March 1979, devolution for Scotland (and Wales) failed to win approval in a referendum, and because of that (and the industrial situation) the Government lost a motion of no-confidence. 'Then an election,' James wrote in his diary on 23 March, 'and if the Conservatives win, what may I expect?' In April, he helped the Conservative candidate in Edinburgh Central, Alex Fletcher, campaign, which brought back memories from Dundee East five years earlier, and watched in the early hours of 5 May as Margaret Thatcher won the election with a good majority. 'So now,' he wondered, 'have I a chance of getting to the Crown Office?'

Unfortunately for James, he was in for another disappointment. After spending several miserable days sitting by his telephone in case a call came from Downing Street, he learned that Nicholas Fairbairn was to be Solicitor General and James Mackay Lord Advocate. He wrote of 'vast disappointment', not least because he had devoted several years to 'struggling in politics' while Mackay, though 'a super-fine lawyer and a man of vast ability' had no political affiliations at all. There was, however, a silver lining: Mackay's appointment meant arrangements had to be made to elect a new Dean of the Faculty and, as James wrote in his diary, 'I hope to have a go for that'.

On 16 May, David Hope formally nominated James as Dean, although it was an unusually competitive election, with four other candidates: the former Solicitor General for Scotland Lord McCluskey, Charles Kemp Davidson QC, Charles R. Macarthur QC and Malcolm Morison QC. 'I hope it is not imprudent of me to stand,' reflected James. 'I am the youngest. But I feel it wise to grab every opportunity that comes.'

But it was not to be, and on 24 May Kemp Davidson emerged the clear winner, with James coming third behind Lord McCluskey. He must have been conscious that his family name had worked against his candidacy: his father had only stood down as Lord President seven years earlier, and his often-tyrannical manner was still, for many, a recent and unhappy memory. This, of course, was deeply unfair to James, whose character – as those such as David Hope who had worked with him knew – was completely different from that of his late father's public (as opposed to softer private) persona. The rather opaque election procedure, in which none of the candidates could play an active role, also did not help.

After the result was announced, James took David Hope for lunch at the New Club ('as a return for his labours'), obviously disappointed but at least more fully aware, as Hope put it, of 'how the land lies'. In September, he also missed out on a part-time position at the Law Commission (which went to John Murray), and so depressed was he that when the new Lord Advocate asked him to reprise his early 1970s role as advocate depute, James demurred. All, however, was not lost, for he was still relatively young in Faculty terms and might yet have another chance to become Dean as, of course, his father and grandfather had been before him. Indeed, later he would console himself

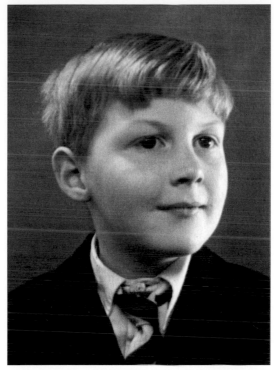

James in Edinburgh Academy school uniform, c. 1940

James with his sister Ann

Graduation, Corpus Christi College, Oxford, 1954

James with his father and mother, James 'Hamish' and Margaret Clyde, 1954

Captain Clyde, National Service

James when he joined the Faculty of Advocates in 1959

James's wedding to Ann Hoblyn, 1963

James with Ann and James 'Hamish' Clyde

The Dundee East general election campaign, 1974

Briglands House, Kinross-shire: the family's country home, 1977

Judge of the Courts of Appeal in Jersey and Guernsey, 1980
(Courtesy of Guernsey Press)

Shiel, the family's new country home, in the early 1980s

Senator of the College of Justice, Scotland, 1985

James and Ann Clyde at the Cyprus Conference of
the Council of Bars and Law Societies of Europe (CCBE)

CCBE dinner, Madrid 1990

James when he received an honorary degree from Heriot-Watt University, 1991

The *Scotsman* front page, 28 October 1992

Receiving an honorary degree from Napier University, 1995
(Courtesy of the *Scotsman*)

Dublin Street home, the New Town, Edinburgh

The garden at Dublin Street, created by James and Ann

Lord of Appeal in Ordinary, 1996 (Courtesy of Universal Press and Agency)

James with Prince Philip, the Duke of Edinburgh, 1993

Relaxing on holiday

Briglands azaleas in the Shiel garden, 2002

The Shiel garden

Tree planting with his grandson James 'Moog' Clyde

Grandchildren Richard, Charles and James ('Moog') Clyde, sons of
Jamie and Emma, taken at Dublin Street, Edinburgh at Christmas 2008, just
before James died.

James's grandchildren, Quentin and Montague ('Monty') Clyde,
sons of Tim and Rebecca, taken in 2018.

James with Tim, Ann and Jamie, 2000

James in his Belfast office as Justice Oversight Commissioner, 2006

James with Ann in the Abercombie Place Gardens, Edinburgh, 2006

that, early in his career, his grandfather had 'had a series of frustrations too'.

In January 1979, there had been a reminder of the first and second Lord Clyde when the Edinburgh Academy extended a unanimous invitation to James to join the school's governing court. He had recently spoken at the Edinburgh Academical Club's 150th anniversary dinner and would become a typically effective team player. Pattie Bell, whose son was at the school, remembers him being very supportive of her idea to make rugby non-compulsory, mainly because rugby-related injuries were then on the rise. 'Right, Pattie,' he told her, 'at the next meeting you be the passion and I'll be the reason.'

It worked, and the sport (which James had disliked during his time at the Academy) ceased to be mandatory. 'James and I would come home together,' Pattie also recalled, 'he was a brilliant mimic and if he laughed at my jokes I felt really proud. I knew him as someone who was great fun, but you always felt when he said something that it carried great authority.' While he would certainly have valued the honour of serving his old school, the subsequent disappointment of gaining neither election to the House of Commons, the (aborted) Scottish Assembly and Dean of the Faculty of Advocates, nor appointment as Lord Advocate, would linger for some time.

In the second half of that year there were some modest consolations. In August, the Home Office invited James to succeed Lord Jauncey (who had recently been appointed to the Scottish Bench) as a Judge of the Courts of Appeal in both Jersey and Guernsey, which meant visiting the Channel Islands once or twice a year for a few days at a time. Although not a senior (or particularly high-profile) position, it was nevertheless a recognition of his legal talents and would do him no harm in progressing, like his predecessor Lord Jauncey, to the Bench in Edinburgh. Lord Hoffmann, a colleague at that time, recalled them both being 'put up in a nice hotel and delivered to the

Court in a very old motorcar of the sort you saw in movies, driven by a man in a peak cap'.

Hogmanay found James in a philosophical mood, and determined to leave behind the 'wild ambitions' of the previous year while still frustrated at being 'in the rut of daily practice'. 'I had thought that this year would bring a change of life,' he reflected in his diary, 'the Crown Office, the Scottish Assembly, the Deanship. But all that has gone. It looks as if the political life is not for me. At least I have my new judicial job in the Channel Islands, and indeed have the papers today for my first appearance there.'

He had been formally appointed to his new position by the Queen on 23 October and was sworn in at two separate ceremonies the following year. In Jersey, the local press misheard the bailiff's reference to James's father having been Lord President of the Court of Session and, much to his amusement, wrote it up as 'the Quarter Session', while in Guernsey his first case involved an appeal against a conviction for importing cannabis. He would spend a lot of his career on the periphery of the British Isles, first in Drumbuie, now in the Channel Islands, and later in Orkney and Northern Ireland.

James would also spend a lot of time on the Continent during the early 1980s. He found himself at the forefront of a sea change within the Scottish legal profession, leading it away from a narrow and parochial view of Scots Law to one more internationally focused and responsive to foreign jurisprudence – even that of England (from 1982 he chaired the Scottish Lawyers' European Group). At Edinburgh University, meanwhile, he played an important part in ensuring that the growing body of European Law became a taught subject, later chairing the Europa Institute, which had been founded in 1968 as a Centre of European Governmental Studies.

But it was via the CCBE that James engaged most actively with legal developments in Europe, representing the Faculty at meetings of the European Bars between 1978 and 1984, and leading the United Kingdom delegation during the second half of that period. The meetings took him all over the Continent: Copenhagen in 1980 (where he was shocked at how expensive dinner was); Bologna in the autumn of 1981; and Paris at the beginning of 1982, where he took a break to watch (with obvious amusement) as President Mitterand was applauded by young lawyers at the Court of Justice. Afterward, he travelled on the Metro, 'clutching my wig and gown', to continue his work at the CCBE.

A plenary meeting in James's home city of Edinburgh in the spring of 1981, however, proved to be his pièce de résistance. He and Ann met the delegates personally at Turnhouse towards the end of April, thereafter organising a visit to Hopetoun House, a reception at Edinburgh Castle and a party at No. 9 Heriot Row. One CCBE delegate, Erik Hermansen, later wrote (in slightly mangled English) that James's 'beautiful dwelling' mirrored his 'generous, open, and sence-of-humour [*sic*] spirits which we have known and appreciated for so long time'. Earlier, David Edward (who had recently stood down as CCBE president) had also written to make James aware 'how much you are respected and liked, and how much your views are relied on, both in the UKD[elegation] and in the C.C.B.E.' Ann, he added, had also 'helped to inject sanity into our disordered male world', and indeed at the party she had looked after the delegates' wives while, as her husband noted proudly in his diary, 'Jamie and Timmy were a great asset and impressed the guests enormously'.

Indeed, whatever the professional frustrations of the last few years James derived considerable joy and comfort from his marriage to Ann and from their two sons, Jamie and Tim, who formed the bedrock to his busy and varied life both within and outside the Law. He was, in short, a devoted family man, most of all at weekends (and during holidays) at Shiel, the 'new' Briglands at Rumbling Bridge.

There he, Ann and the boys enjoyed an outdoor life, digging, lighting bonfires, planting and tending trees, and gradually transforming a patch of woodland into a three-acre garden. 'He loved being outdoors, but only for the dirtiest of jobs or in the roughest of weather would he <u>not</u> wear a tie,' Jamie recalled at his father's memorial service. 'As we headed back to the city on a Sunday evening, we always returned with a sense of achievement, even if we had only succeeded in relocating a rhododendron for the third time.' (After visiting an oil rig in 1983, James even kept hold of his orange safety clothes and boots, knowing they would come in handy for the garden at Briglands.)

On one Sunday morning in March 1979 Anne (later Lady) Smith recalls finding James and Ann on her doorstep with a gift of eggs from Briglands as a thank-you present. A few days earlier, she had encountered 'two distressed boys' outside her home in Edinburgh's Royal Crescent. She remembered:

> They explained that they lived on Heriot Row and that some other boys had been chasing after them. So, I took them in, Jamie and Timothy, then walked them up to the corner of Heriot Row. I then thought nothing more about it. At the time, I was in the second year of an apprenticeship at Shepherd and Wedderburn and five weeks earlier I'd begun going out with a partner who then proposed to me. It was the morning after he asked me to marry him that I found the Clydes on my doorstep, only then did I make the connection with the two distressed boys. They [James and Ann] were terribly kind and invited me round.

A few months later, Jamie Clyde acted as a page at Anne's wedding at St Giles' Cathedral in Edinburgh. 'He was superb,' James wrote in his diary. 'Stood absolutely still (with his feet together) and did all the right things. I was so proud of him.'

Lady Smith also recalled seeing James reading a Shakespeare play in his chambers 'because one of his sons was reading it or appearing in it and he wanted to help him'. She would be among guests at No. 9 Heriot Row invited to watch Jamie and Tim perform in their own theatrical productions, but at other times there was a more formal atmosphere, for although James was sociable, generally a kindly, humorous man with an infectious laugh, he was not by inclination very gregarious.

Jamie also recalled his father working from his study (known as 'The Library') amid towering piles of papers and two walls lined floor-to-ceiling with books, many of which had belonged to his father:

> Often there would be 'consultations' which would mean the library door was firmly closed. The consequence of an interruption by my brother or I were never specified but were clearly understood. Perhaps that is why the first words I apparently uttered were 'shut the door!' When the meetings broke up, Tim and I were to be neither seen nor heard as the group of serious looking suits passed through the hallway to leave. Only when the front door was closed, could we run into the smoke-filled Library to see Dad.

David Hope recalls that it was generally expected that advocates would have a consulting area like James's library, a large room at the front of their house where they could meet clients and colleagues.

It was a civilised way of life. Court finished (as it still does) at 4pm, enabling judges and their counsel (many of whom lived in the 'Square Mile') to be home half an hour later, where they would carry on working. Following a consultation, Lord Mackenzie-Stuart, who had influenced James's European outlook, if not his style of advocacy, was known for asking visitors to linger a little longer to discuss an 'urgent matter', which was code for a glass of sherry and a cigarette. 'James didn't have sherry or cigarettes,' recalled Hope, 'but he did have a lovely coal fire, and it was always a delight to sit next to that in an easy chair in his library.'

Once business was concluded, Jamie and Tim eagerly anticipated their father's bedtime stories, which typically involved a character known as 'Mr Pumplechook' and his collection of crazy companions whose adventures were carefully woven around what had happened to them that day. 'It was not until Dad's storytelling was revived for the new generation of grandsons', Jamie later reflected, 'that I fully appreciated the hidden moral messages that Dad cleverly embedded into each story.' Unfortunately, they were never written down.

As the two boys prepared for bed, they would hear the front door slam as a courier from Parliament House (known as the 'Bag Man'), with his jailer's ring of advocates' door keys, dropped off the papers for the following morning's cases in a leather bag the size of a bin liner. 'This signalled the start of Dad's night shift to prepare for court in the morning,' recalled Jamie. 'This seemingly endless homework was much worse than that given to Tim & me by our teachers – perhaps it was a reason why neither of us chose to go into the Law!'

Later both James's sons became conscious that their father had largely kept them in the dark as to the nature of his working life, and perhaps deliberately so, determined they would both pursue their own hopes and aspirations free of familial and legal expectations. 'In his modest way, he never persuaded us to do anything he wanted,' recalled Tim. 'He encouraged us to find our own path and seemed to be proud of everything we did – including travelling around playing the drums in a band or working for British Rail – hardly the stuff a traditional judge would aspire to for his sons!'

And when it came to discipline, James never shouted at his sons when they were naughty (in fact, he rarely got visibly angry about anything), but the sense they might have disappointed him was far more motivating. 'If there ever was a family argument,' remembered Tim, 'Dad would sit there and listen, then after a while when it seemed there was no resolution one of us would realise that he hadn't commented and ask him for his view. He would say three words and the answer was clear. Debate resolved.'

James's temperament was sustained by a deep religious faith, which was obvious from an article he had written to mark the centenary of the Episcopalian (or Anglican) St Mary's Cathedral (a locus for several generations of the Clyde family) in October 1979. He reflected on its value to a congregation that shared the 'particular sense of belonging which comes from familiarity with regular worship and association with each other', and also its wider value to the diocese 'as the mother church of all the congregations' and to the public at large 'as a monument of architectural importance and as a statement of our Christian faith'.

He had served on the Cathedral vestry, later becoming the first chairman of its Pastoral Link Visiting Scheme and patron of the Friends of St Mary's Cathedral. James's advice was also sought on many of the Church's wider concerns, his expertise on questions of property and trust law proving particularly valuable. 'His contribution was quite substantial, and he made it out of conviction,' reflected Graham Forbes, later Provost of St Mary's Cathedral. 'It wasn't paid – he gave up many fee-paying opportunities!'

In 1976, James had become a trustee of St Mary's Music School, which had been created several years earlier out of the original Cathedral Choir School. In this, he played a part in maintaining a tradition of church choral music which was close to his heart and the school, and indeed his son Tim would later become a chorister there. This was a big part of the Clydes' family life, for the children were required to sing six days a week.

This spirit of public service also drove James's role as Chancellor to the Bishop of Argyll (to whom he gave sound counsel in

times of difficulty, not least as a trustee for the Cathedral and
College of the Holy Spirit on the Island of Cumbrae), and no
matter how busy he was at Parliament House, he gave freely of
his time to a number of charitable and educational organisations, more often than not gratis. In 1983, for example, he had
helped compile a report on the 'Future Role and Activities of
the Council of West End Churches', for which came thanks
from St Cuthbert's Parish Church. 'The report itself is a masterly
document', wrote a grateful minister, 'and is, without doubt,
the product of considerable thought, research and not a little
imagination.'

> Acute, incisive thinking, probing and penetrating the
> wooliness of aim and purpose, was what we in CWEC
> were looking for and I can assure you that you certainly
> fulfilled our expectations. To compile such a compre-
> hensive report will have involved considerable sacrifice
> of time and energy on the part of yourself and your
> colleagues – we do appreciate, therefore, the fact that
> you went the second mile on our behalf.

James's committee had even been nicknamed 'The Three Wise
Men' although, added the priest, 'you can rest assured that
we stopped short of referring to you as Caspar, Melchior and
Balthasar'. It was another indication that he was immensely well
liked, not least because he never paraded his intellect.

Politically, James was a small 'c' conservative but pragmatic
(thus his support for Scottish devolution, not yet a mainstream
view), decades of travel and experience of humanity good and
bad (via his legal work) having taught him always to look for the
good in a situation, person or even country, however unpleasant
it might at first appear. After holidaying in what was then still
Yugoslavia in the summer of 1982, for example, he was genuinely interested to experience the 'progress' of a 'Socialist state'.
'A liberal regime with little evidence of oppression,' he reflected

in his diary. 'While the people seemed not too friendly or happy, they were of a dour . . . character anyway.' Ann remembered the food being basic and lacking choice. James, for example, ordered 'fruit compote' for breakfast, only to find it consisted of a bowl of water containing a single prune, apricot and grape.

Closer to home, James was also determined that Scots Law – which he regularly feared was under threat from inferior English practice – be available as widely, and affordably, as possible. With that goal in mind, from 1980 he chaired the Scottish Consumer Council's Class Actions Working Party, which in October 1982 published calls for the law to be changed in order that a single civil or 'class' action might take the place of several individual claims for reparation arising from the same circumstances. He anticipated opposition, particularly within the Faculty, but James had no doubts class actions would benefit ordinary people from all walks of life, and not just those with means.

More prosaically, the early 1980s was taken up with the Valuation Appeal Court, Medical Appeal Tribunals and apparently endless Procedure Roll debates (at which the legal basis of a claim was tested in arguments from both sides), little of which James found especially stimulating, although perhaps surprisingly he considered his duties as chairman of the Potato Marketing Board's disciplinary committee 'great fun'. And when Nicholas Fairbairn was compelled to resign as Solicitor General in early 1982 following both legal and personal indiscretions, it rekindled hopes of a Crown Office appointment.

'I see indications in the paper that the new solicitor-general will be outside Parliament – Kenny Cameron . . . and David Edward are mentioned,' he wrote in his diary on 23 January. 'Why not me? Pride severely damaged and I feel really quite depressed. I suppose I should have accepted James Mackay's initiative to be a[n advocate] depute years ago but I did do that before and I am the only one who has stood for Parliament at least. I begin to wonder whether I should not cut loose altogether.'

Of course James did not actually want to become Solicitor

General, a position both his father and grandfather had held, but rather Lord Advocate or Dean of the Faculty, both of which would have increased his prospects of becoming the third Clyde as Lord President. On that occasion, everyone was surprised when Peter Fraser, the Conservative MP for South Angus, succeeded Fairbairn as Solicitor General, but the point was that James's name no longer seemed to be in the mix.

When Lady Carmont, the wife of Lord Carmont, a long-standing judge until his death in 1965, passed away in September 1983, James wrote sadly that 'another of the few old figures of my childhood disappears'. He remembered visits to their house in North Berwick and to Loch Awe, 'the dinners and lunches at Heriot Row and at the Avenue Greenhill Gardens, their last home', where Lady Carmont had 'lived a widow for some 20 years surrounded with the very greatest of valuable paintings and pieces'.

The following month, James attended the opening of the 'Legal Year' ceremony at Westminster Abbey, and afterwards 'the Lord Chancellor's breakfast (the unsocial crush in the House of Lords with little to eat or drink) and the weary procession at the Law Courts for the formal opening'. At around the same time, Charles Kemp Davidson, who had beaten him in the election for Dean four years earlier, was appointed to the Bench, thus creating a vacancy to lead the Faculty. James decided to have another go despite having few keen supporters beyond his clerk Colin Fox (who did not have a vote), and although David Hope once again agreed to nominate him, he did so warning that James might come last.

Although his father's reign as Lord President was by 1983 a fading memory, that posed another challenge to James's candidacy for Dean; the Faculty was much bigger by then and while the older advocates still feared another Clyde in a position of authority, the younger advocates knew of neither Hamish's reputation nor his son's good work in the decade since his father had retired. And while James still felt the weight of expectation (even though his parents had passed away several years before), he could not bring himself *not* to stand, despite Hope's well-intentioned caution.

When the election was held in November 1983, James came fifth, thus ending any prospect of becoming Dean, having stood and lost twice in the space of four years. Several colleagues wrote to commiserate, including one who had no doubt he would 'rise above this disappointment . . . and perhaps it may help to know that your friends share it'. Of course, it was difficult for James to think in those terms, particularly as he and others considered him eminently suited to the role. 'He'd have been a good figurehead of the Bar because he had such an attractive personality' was David Hope's view. 'But others didn't see it that way. It was all very political and depended upon luck and events as much as talent.'

Shortly before Christmas, the English QC David Calcutt, who had worked with James as a member of the UK's delegation to the CCBE, also tried to cheer him up: 'Don't worry about the Faculty: it won't make the slightest difference to your ultimate career. It needs an Englishman to see it clearly.' That much was true, although 1984 brought further upheaval when James Mackay, Lord Advocate since 1979, moved from the Crown Office to the Bench. James, Ann and several of their friends hoped that his time had finally come, something fuelled by press speculation (which invariably turned out to be wrong) that suggested either he or his friend Kenny Cameron might succeed Mackay.

But on returning home on 16 May 1984, James heard that Cameron had been appointed Lord Advocate. 'It was as I had feared,' he wrote in his diary, 'but the end of a last hope is fearfully depressing, and I really am low.'

> I have been waiting and hoping for so long for something – the Deanship or the Advocate. Now I have lost both for ever. And though I shouldn't think it, it

does seem odd. I thought I had all the qualifications for
the office. I even stood for Parliament. But there it is.
I just wonder how They, whoever They are, came to
make this choice. And why, when I was obviously in
the running, I was rejected. Oh dear. I do feel rejected.
And I just can't face going on in practice year after year
getting older and older and getting precisely nowhere.
True, there is Jersey. I must have been thought good
enough for that. And surely, I have some ability. So
why do I lose out every time?

He then packed for a trip to Amsterdam, 'fed up and depressed',
which was understandable in the circumstances. Once again,
friends wrote to share in his disappointment, including a neighbour who believed 'one day the tide must flow strongly in the
direction you are intended to go'. Cameron's appointment as
Lord Advocate did create some movement, with James succeed-
ing his friend as chairman of the Committee of Investigation for
Scotland (an agricultural marketing body which rarely met) and
the Milk Marketing Board, but it was scant compensation for yet
another professional disappointment.

But David Calcutt's prediction, that his failure to become
Dean would not make 'the slightest difference' to his ultimate
career, was ultimately proven correct. In February 1985, as James
acted on behalf of the Cockburn Association in objecting to the
proposed Western Relief Road, Malcolm Morison QC replaced
Lord Ross in the Court of Session, and since it was likely
another sitting judge would soon retire, the *Scotsman* speculated
that 'Mr Clyde's appointment would be widely welcomed at the
Bar as a further strengthening of the Scottish Bench'. Likewise,
the *Glasgow Herald* reported 'talk of a third Lord Clyde on the
Bench', his abilities as an advocate being 'held in high regard'.

James had recently turned 53 ('My goodness' was his diarised
response) and on 23 July he went to see his old friend Kenny
Cameron (the new Lord Advocate) at the Crown Office. 'He

offered me a seat on the Bench and I accepted,' he later wrote in his diary. 'I cannot believe it. Having thought about it for so long the reality does not seem real.' Although it was not yet in the public domain, he could tell Ann and celebrated over lunch with her and Jamie. He also started to clear out old papers, still not quite believing 'that the end of practice has come'. When in August a colleague asked him about media speculation to the effect that James was destined for the Bench, he 'gave nothing away'.

Even colleagues such as David Hope had no inkling of the news, although movements on the Bench, which had begun with Lord Fraser's retirement from the House of Lords (as one of two Scottish Lords of Appeal in Ordinary), meant vacancies would arise, not least because in August Lord Wheatley retired as Lord Justice Clerk and was succeeded by Lord Ross. Finally, word reached Hope, but he kept schtum. 'As it happened I was working closely with James on the updating of Armour for its first release, and we were all invited to Briglands for lunch on Sunday,' he recorded in his diary on 10 September.

> But then James and Ann very kindly told us about it themselves while we were walking at Rumbling Bridge in the inevitable pouring rain. Today at last this news also, with that of Lord Cameron's retirement after 30 years on the bench and 20 years in the First Division, is in the newspapers. James Clyde's appointment gives the greatest pleasure by far. He is such a fine and lively person. He has been so hurt by disappointments over the years that it is marvellous that he can now be settled in to realise his full potential. It has not been easy for him being his father's and grandfather's child, but at least he has found his place with them – and how nice it is that he has done so as Lord Cameron's replacement.

On 9 September, as James spent the day 'finishing up ends of work', he watched news of his appointment on the television and began receiving letters of congratulations almost right away. Some were almost as excited as James must have been. 'Happy days!' proclaimed his colleague David Maxwell. 'It must be a great relief to be freed from the trials and tribulations of practice. But you were a Happy Warrior!' Lord Allanbridge, meanwhile, deployed a classical allusion, writing that 'just as the Roman Legionnaires cried "Africa! Africa! when they returned to "the South" and the sun and the glory of Italy after years in the North, so I cry "At last! At last!"'

David Hope (who was to inherit some of James's valuation and trust work, as well as 'his locker in the inner sanctum of the gown room') sent a map, which included Briglands, to furnish James's new judicial office, adding that his pleasure at the news 'outshines <u>by far</u> the many other events of this remarkable summer'. David Edward also referred to his countryside retreat, speculating that 'the vistas opening out of relaxed weekends at Briglands must be of a more than usually roseate hue, not to speak of <u>real</u> vacations'. He continued:

> The relief of getting off the P. H. [Parliament House] treadmill is enormous, as I know (in spite of having, apparently, exchanged one for another!), and . . . what is more, both of us can, with rather more honesty and confidence than is sometimes the case, say that we know James will be a superb judge and, in spite of what I say about my treadmill (which is decidedly more congenial) my only regret is that I won't have the pleasure of appearing before him.

Such enthusiasm reflected shared frustration among friends that James's advancement had not come sooner. On the morning of 10 September, he held a final consultation then celebrated over lunch (and supper) with Ann and the boys. 'The news is in the *Scotsman* and congratulations are coming in,' he wrote in his diary. 'Kathleen Dunpark (was Macfie) looked in in a state of high excitement and pleasure. Colin Fox called and carried off the last of my papers.'[1]

A week later James was fitted 'with breeches, buckles and stockings' for his installation as a Senator of the College of Justice, which took place before Lord President Emslie on 2 October, an event he described at length in his diary:

> Manson (the Faculty Servant) called for me at 9.30. I was dressed in court dress, black breaches, silk stockings and buckled shoes, court coat with lace frill and lace cuffs. My wig awaited me, and white gloves in the judge's rooms. The other judges came in as I waited and eventually I followed their procession into the First Division when I walked down to the floor of the Court, handed up my Warrant which was then read by the Principal Clerk, all standing. Then I took two oaths, standing with my right hand raised while Lord President Emslie pronounced the oaths. Then I signed the two oaths on large parchment sheets, with a pen kindly provided, and remembering to recover my gloves. Then my judicial gown was put on and the President invited me [to] take my seat. I walked up to the bench, shook hands with all the judges and reached the empty chair at the end of the bench. I bowed to the judges, to the spectators and to the family who were sitting in the little special box at the side – Sweetie [Ann] and the boys (both specially off school).

Mary Hope was also in the jury box, which her husband David called 'a place of honour' in his diarised account of the

---

1 Kathleen was a Heriot Row neighbour and by this time wife of Lord Dunpark, making her Lady Dunpark; both widowed, they had married that year.

proceedings. 'James himself was in the best of form, firm, polite, immaculate and deeply happy,' he wrote. 'It was a ceremony of real polish which ended with a feeling that the Bench had acquired someone of real calibre.'

Back at Heriot Row James posed for press photographs then went for a 'very expensive lunch at the George Hotel with the ladies', and Tim (Jamie had gone back to school). 'It is hard to believe it has all happened,' reflected the third Lord Clyde in his diary. 'But I am now a judge.'

Chapter 6

The Third Lord Clyde

The judicial oath James took on his appointment to the Court of Session spoke of doing 'right by all manner of people without fear or favour, affection or ill-will', a philosophy he had always applied professionally and would continue to do so now he was a Senator of the College of Justice. He also brought other qualities to the Bench, chiefly patience and courtesy, which made him a sharp contrast to his more abrasive and mischievous father.

A photograph carried by several newspapers after he died reflected these characteristics, showing – as Kenny Cameron put it – James 'seated, leaning slightly forward, one hand raised to his chin and a gentle, almost quizzical smile on his face, clearly listening intently to what was being said to him'. As ever, he possessed a sharp legal mind, quick to grasp the essence of a case while putting nervous counsel and witnesses at their ease. Few doubted his humanity or impartiality. 'He was a very good example of how to be a good, fair judge and how to help those appearing in front of him help him,' recalled Anne Smith. 'If you're tetchy and sarcastic you'll close down counsel, but he had this lovely laugh. You could hear it come before him – a very honest laugh.'

Similarly, Tim Clyde recalled his father's laugh as 'genuine – not the kind of laugh one puts on following a mediocre joke. It came from the depth of his heart.'

He was a genuinely happy man who loved the people around him [and] had a hugely engaging nature. He seemed to click with everybody – from a fellow European judge to the local newsagent. He was genuinely interested in everyone he met. But this did lead to an issue – remembering everyone he met. I recall one occasion walking around the New Town with Jamie and my dad and we bumped into a jolly chap who greeted Dad with 'Hello, James' and the two of them carried out an enthusiastic conversation for almost five minutes with much laughter and familiar jokes. Finally, when we walked on my brother asked Dad 'Who was that?' to which Dad replied 'I haven't the foggiest!'

This sense of humour, remembered Tim, also had a 'naughty, intelligent and flippant side'. 'Despite the seriousness of much of his work, he realised that nothing should be taken too seriously.' Tim also recalled

one time when I must have been around 16, we were checking in at Edinburgh Airport and faced by a particularly self-important security official. He predictably asked 'Did you pack these bags yourself?' to which Dad and I nodded. He then said 'Have you been asked to take anything by anyone else?' and I looked at Dad who smiled cheekily and said 'No, except for the bombs and drugs!' Now, had it been after 9/11 or anyone else who had said that, we probably would have spent a night in jail, but with Dad's charm we managed to get away with the self-important security man smiling slightly and saying 'Sir, you should know better!'

James's unassuming nature also endured despite his elevation to the Bench. When Pattie Bell happened to mention to the owner of Lastingham Grange, a hotel in North Yorkshire, that Lord

Clyde had recently been his guest, it turned out James had simply given his name, more modestly, as 'Mr Clyde'. So, the next time he and Ann stayed there the owner made a great fuss as if he were minor royalty, something James found as embarrassing as he did amusing.

James's promotion compelled him to give up other positions, for example as Chancellor to the Bishop of Argyll and the Isles, his duties as a judge in Guernsey and Jersey, and his chairmanship of the Medical Appeals Tribunal. And, of course, it did not mean he abandoned his ambition to become Lord President, indeed he was confident Lord Emslie's successor would be selected from among those on the Bench and thus continued a friendly rivalry with long-standing colleagues like Kenny Cameron, David Hope and David Edward, none of whom were yet on the Bench. Significantly, although he was the third of his family to take the judicial title of Lord Clyde, neither his father nor his grandfather had served as Senators, so already his career had begun to follow a different path.

On 3 October 1985, James sat as a judge for the first time, working late on several petitions and divorces, including one pursuer who, to his amusement, was the mother of a boy (presumably a friend of his sons) who was coming to stay at No. 9 Heriot Row that evening. Edinburgh was a small city and its legal fraternity even more so. James kept a newspaper cutting marked 'my first case', a ruling against petitioners from a bankrupt confectionery company who were trying to prevent a BBC broadcast concerning their business.

Several days later, James also experienced his first sitting in a criminal court, although much of his work as a judge would concern civil matters. The tenor of his diary during this period noticeably brightens, and he was obviously in his element after almost a decade full of political and legal setbacks. In the autumn of 1985, he composed some verse welcoming his colleague William Prosser (another Edinburgh Academical) to the Bench, which captured something of an irreverent streak well known to his close friends and family:

> May I set your mind
> At rest. The Senate you will find
> Is fully manned not just by me
> But by the judges twenty-three,
> All kind, compassionate and caring,
> All their tiny salaries sharing,
> Long-life cream of the profession,
> Loved of counsel, Lords of Session.
> Janice Webster must have thought
> That Lords Clyde sat in every court;
> But I assure you in this rhyme
> They only come one at a time.

Others responded in kind, including this obviously affectionate poem from May Rodger, one of his secretaries:

> James Clyde, you're tall with wavy hair
> So handsome and so debonair.
> And when you thrill me with your smile.
> I get all mixed up with my files.
> My heart goes pitter patter pitter.
> Whenever you dictate a letter.
> Please make me happy, drop a line,
> And say you'll be my Valentine.

And having grown bored with the often-prosaic routine of daily practice, James now found himself dealing with substantial – and potentially far-reaching – cases. In June 1986, for example, a French national who had been refused a student grant by the Scottish Education Department became the first case referred by the Court of Session (i.e. Lord Clyde) to the European Court of Justice in Luxembourg. With his expertise in European Law, it was apt that such a decision fell to James, a veteran of several CCBE meetings earlier that decade. Later, he would even remark that if he were starting his career then (rather than in 1959) he might have taken 'advantage of the opportunities offered by the European community', just as his former devil-master Lord Mackenzie-Stuart and friend David Edward had done.

James also found himself engaging with matters involving the media, both broadcasting and the printed press, and he generally took an enlightened view, perhaps a subconscious attempt to shake off the legacy of his father as Lord President, who had interpreted the law of contempt of court (as it affected journalists) with particular severity. Even after a UK statute had come into force in 1981, Scottish judges had continued to take a much more restrictive view than their English counterparts, but together with Lord Emslie (still Lord President) James took a different approach.

His most significant judgement in that context, given in November 1986, concerned a former advocate called David Cunningham, who had sued the *Scotsman, Dundee Courier* and *Glasgow Herald* for £600,000 damages, claiming they had defamed him in their coverage of an interim interdict hearing in March 1984 by Lord Cameron. Reports in all three newspapers had contained allegations from the summons, which crucially had not been read out in court and were therefore – in Cunningham's contention – not covered by privilege.

The newspapers, however, argued that as the summons was before the court and referred to (though not in full) by counsel, then it was covered, along with oral statements, by the usual rules of qualified privilege. Having reviewed a century of pertinent cases, James upheld the newspapers' plea, arguing that a distinction could not be made between written and oral submissions given that both formed an intrinsic part of the case. But further to that, he articulated a more general view that it was important for public confidence in the Scottish justice system for the public to 'be able to see and hear the proceedings for themselves'. He continued:

> They must be able to attend a court and see and hear what goes on. But their attendance will be of little point if the proceedings are so conducted that the communications made in open court between counsel and the Judge are not disclosed. If the public are to be informed of the proceedings, the proceedings ought to be intelligible. If justice is to be seen to be done, what is done must be open to inspection. The public must have at least the opportunity of understanding what is going on and if they do not have the opportunity I do not consider that the hearing is a public one. If the hearing is a public hearing then it does not seem to me that characteristic is destroyed simply because, for perfectly proper reasons of convenience, a document is referred to and not read out in full.

James's decision set a precedent still followed thirty years later. The *Scotsman's* law correspondent, George Saunders, praised his 'exhaustive examination' of qualified privilege in the reporting of court hearings as 'one of the most important pronouncements on Press freedom for nearly a century'. But it did not mean James believed in giving journalists a free reign. At another hearing, he cautioned newspaper headline writers against sensationalism having cleared the *Dunfermline Press and West of Fife Advertiser* of an allegation of contempt brought by the defence in a murder trial. While the article itself had been 'an unimpeachable piece of accurate and correct reporting up to the high standards we are used to from Scottish reporters', the headline – exaggerated to capture attention – had not.

There was, after all, ink in the Clyde blood, and on 30 January 1987 James saw a portrait of John McDermott, a former newspaper editor and ancestor, while visiting Dumfries to speak at a Burns Supper (the portrait had been gifted to the municipal chambers by his late father).[1] The next day, a Saturday, he received an urgent call to consider an interim interdict (or injunction) against a search warrant by the BBC in Glasgow. Special Branch had dramatically descended on the broadcaster's office looking for evidence of a breach of the Official Secrets Act. The *Sunday Times* later splashed on James's decision to suspend the warrant (on the grounds it had been too wide in scope) during a special sitting, which meant film cans and documents taken by police officers had to be returned to the BBC.

As James's judicial oath had stipulated, he was to do 'right by all manner of people without fear or favour' – even if that meant the police. In dealing with criminal cases he would often suffer criticism for lenience in sentencing, although that ignored an understanding of human frailty[2] and what Kenny Cameron called 'a profound desire to bring about reformation of the guilty rather than look for retribution'. This was clear from James's account of a visit he and other judges had made to a couple of prisons in March 1986. First, they inspected Saughton in Edinburgh, which he noted was 'clean and depressing', but 'far from inhuman so far as the facilities were concerned'.

But when the group moved on to a detention centre near Alloa, his mood changed, its 'quasi-military training routine' bringing back memories of his basic training during National Service.

We saw the young men drilling and training around a gymnasium and their cells all mostly rejuvenated with the blankets folded into a rectangular pile with the

---

1   James owned a whisky glass given by Burns' wife Jean Armour to his ancestor John McDiarmid, a friend of the poet, as well as silhouettes of Burns and Armour, James Glencairn Burns and William Nicol Burns.

2   Another of James's many voluntary positions was vice president of Edinburgh's Royal Blind Asylum and School from 1987.

sheets sandwiched in between and two shirts laid out
neatly creased, and the floor immensely polished . . .
All just like the barracks at basic training. But there
was something oppressive about the place. The young
offenders' bit was a little more constructive. But a fearful lot of pressure and remoteness and lack of human
contact. I was rather depressed when I got home.

It spoke well of James that he did not completely detach himself
from the consequences of the sentencing he and his colleagues
handed down from the Bench. Another incident in the summer
of 1987 – though stressful at the time – also revealed his tremendous professional integrity. In any other context, a parking
fine such as that incurred by him while shopping in Stockbridge
would have been little more than an irritation, but for James
it induced panic. 'I explained what I was doing and they [the
police] were sympathetic with a judge being an offender,' he
later wrote in his diary. 'I was between the studs at the lights
which is evidently illegal. They cautioned me and I couldn't
think what to say if anything.' But he told the police they would
have to report the incident, his first offence.

Later the police rang James to say they felt compelled to
report the case to the fiscal, and he called on the Lord President
with the intention of standing down. 'He said it was of no
importance and I should not worry and certainly should not
resign,' he told his diary, but nevertheless he was 'furious' with
himself. It was, as Lord Emslie had realised, a storm in a teacup.
James paid his £24 fine at Edinburgh District Court and, luckily, the press did not make the connection between 'James John
Clyde' the private citizen, and 'Lord Clyde' the judge.

Life on the Bench, meanwhile, was rarely without incident.
In September 1987, James was sitting at the High Court in
Dumfries when a man accused of murder produced a knife and
tried to stab himself in the witness box. 'If you want blood,' he

shouted, 'I'll give you blood.' 'There was panic in the jury box,' James recounted in his diary. 'A policeman pounced on him and held him on the floor. I adjourned and we waited while everything calmed down. Then the Crown accepted his plea of guilty and we all went home.'

James also found himself in the newspapers when an acquaintance of Jamie (by then at the Edinburgh Academy Upper School) admitted stealing several cheques, a bank card and other documents from their Heriot Row home. In December 1988, he left the court of his alma mater, Edinburgh Academy, to become Chairman of the Council of St George's School for Girls, maintaining his long-standing interest in education with additional duties as a governor of Napier Polytechnic (soon to become a university) and a member of the governing body of Edinburgh University as Chancellor's Assessor on the University Court.

At the beginning of 1988, James had attended, along with three other judicial graduates of Corpus Christi (William Prosser, Lord Coulsfield and Lord Dervaird) and Lord Cameron of Lochbroom (Kenny Cameron, the Lord Advocate), a special dinner at Oxford University held in their honour. 'The President proposed our healths, I replied for the guests and proposed a toast to the Lord Chancellor who came as a guest,' James wrote in his diary, a reference to his old Rating Valuation colleague James Mackay, who had joined Margaret Thatcher's Cabinet in 1987.[3] He worked tremendously hard on his speech, which he thought 'went down well enough', then staying up till after 2am chatting with dozens of other guests.

As David Edward had predicted on James's promotion to the Bench in 1985, being a judge would afford more time for relaxation in addition to the rigours of the circuit. When it came to work in general he did not shirk, progressing from a member

---

3   In June 1989, James was also in attendance when James Mackay was introduced as an honorary member of the Speculative Society.

to chairman of the Scottish Valuation Advisory Committee in 1987 (later contributing an article as the leading expert on Valuation to the new Stair Memorial Encyclopaedia of the Laws of Scotland), and writing frequent reviews of legal tomes including the Stair Encyclopaedia.

The late 1980s was a period of considerable upheaval in Scots Law, with the Government's Law Reform (Miscellaneous Provisions) (Scotland) Bill proving controversial (as were equivalent reforms in England promoted by James Mackay), chiefly by widening the provision of legal services. One legal academic even said it should be called the Scots Law (Abolition) Bill, 'because that indicates its object and probable effect'. James had always been alive to potential threats – mainly from south of the border – to the distinct traditions of the Scottish legal system, albeit far from an uncritical admirer.

In a speech at Strathclyde University at the beginning of 1989, he got some flak after suggesting aspects of Scots civil law failed to meet the requirements of the European Convention on Human Rights (specifically Article 6, that citizens receive 'a fair and public hearing in a reasonable time'), adding that the potentially huge expense of taking civil action to obtain damages was a major deterrent to all but the very rich or the very poor (who would receive legal aid).

Embarrassed by the press coverage, James stressed that he had been speaking in a personal capacity, although the new Lord Advocate, Peter Fraser, whom he had congratulated by letter, replied to say his comments had 'struck a chord'. James frequently gave speeches, including one to the Scottish Young Lawyers Association (of which he was president), 'an attempt to stir them into interest and effort for the new Europe', particularly as the Community prepared to be reborn as the 'European Union' in 1992, generating more and more distinctly European law in the process. Despite this feeling of legal flux, he still believed (as he told new members of the Bar) 'independence, integrity, courage, honesty, energy and conscientiousness' were 'the traditional hallmarks of the greatest advocate', as much at the end of the 1980s as in the late 1950s when he had been in their shoes.

There were also changes at Parliament House in the summer of 1989, prompted by the retirement of Lord Emslie after seventeen years in charge of the Bench. For years James had been tipped – by journalists and colleagues – as a third-generation successor as Lord President, other names in the mix including Kenny Cameron and Lord Ross (as Lord Justice Clerk, the second most senior judge). And he had long dreamed of reached this professional 'summit', 'the job I have lived for', even allowing himself 'so many reckless thoughts of what I would and could do if I held it' (such as the creation of a Third Division).

But on 7 August, just after an interdict hearing at Parliament House, James learned that David Hope was to succeed Emslie, a 'bolt from the blue' that left him 'duly crushed'. The decision was certainly a surprise, for not only was Hope only fifty-one, making him the youngest ever Lord President, but he lacked judicial experience, not being a Senator of the College of Justice (but having served as Dean of the Faculty since 1986). He was also a friend, and someone James rated highly, but that could not prevent a 'fearful sense of disappointment'. 'This does seem', he wrote sadly in his diary, 'to be the end of the road.'

Although, like James, one of Hope's ancestors had also been Lord President, that had been in the early nineteenth century and cast nothing like the shadow of Hamish Clyde. It seemed there was still a widespread feeling, just as there had been in the late 1970s, that another Clyde in a senior position would have been too much of a succession, and too soon. Of course, few doubted that as a judge James was of a high calibre, but in reality – and although his name was one of three considered by the Government – it is likely the real choice had actually been between Hope and Lord Ross. The Prime Minister (Margaret Thatcher) then had to choose between the perceived establishment candidate (Ross) and a potential reformer, so naturally she opted for Hope.

Helping her decide would have been the key triumvirate of Lord Fraser (the Lord Advocate), Malcolm Rifkind (the Secretary of State for Scotland) and Lord Mackay (the Lord Chancellor), with the first taking the lead and consulting with the outgoing Lord President and Lord Justice Clerk. Understandably, James turned over in his mind a number of explanations, including the possibility that the Lord Chancellor had expressed a preference for his former devil at the Scottish Bar, David Hope. Lord Emslie later told James he had arranged with the Lords Mackay and Fraser for him as successor and believed it had all been settled, but this simply reopened James's 'wounds of disappointment'. Even worse, the gloom pervaded during his and Ann's wedding anniversary as well as a family holiday in Corsica. Back at Parliament House, James took care to appear cheerful, but inwardly he was dreading the prospect of another decade as a Senator of the College of Justice, worried that the CCBE and his involvement with schools and universities might stand as his 'only achievement', 'creeping quietly to retirement without having held one office, one post of any responsibility'.

Poignantly, on 11 August James had to sit 'in the Lord President's chair' for a hearing in the First Division and shortly after wrote a 'very kind and generous letter' of congratulations to Hope. On 29 September he watched as David was installed as Lord President. 'It seems all unreal,' he wrote in his diary. 'But there it is. The thing is done. One must plough on.' James had always been a worrier – colleagues remember the phrases 'dearie oh' or 'dearie me' punctuating his conversation, which in his diary became simply 'oh dear'. But while the shock of missing out on the Lord Presidency lingered longer than previous disappointments over the Lord Advocacy and Deanship, eventually the mood lifted – aided by Ann and the boys – and he became more philosophical. Perhaps, he mused at one point, it constituted 'the darkest hour before the dawn?'

Chapter 7

There Is More in Life Than the Law

As 1989 drew to its end, two conversations with close colleagues helped cheer James up: William Prosser's friendly suggestion that they were now in competition for appointment as a Law Lord, an impression confirmed by his former clerk, Colin Fox. 'Colin told me how people had been asking him how I had taken the news of David Hope's appointment – that I was looking cheerful – and was I really,' he noted in his diary on 1 November. 'He also said that someday I would go to London. There was talk of Harry Keith retiring. So, I started the day with a little jollity.'

The well-respected Keith had served as one of two Scottish Law Lords since 1977, although talk of his standing down proved premature. Nevertheless, the 1990s would prove a varied and ultimately satisfying decade for James. For the time being, however, he would serve on the Bench, where he remained a popular presence – both in and out of court – on account of his courteousness and the scrupulous care with which he attended to submissions. He displayed particular commitment to often long and complex tax and civil cases, once memorably interpreting the meaning of the word 'storm' in a disputed insurance policy.

There were changes, meanwhile, in the Court of Session. In January 1990 Ranald MacLean was sworn in as a new judge, taking the place of Ian Murray (Lord Dervaird) who had resigned the previous month following allegations concerning his private life. 'There has been a great scandal since then that four other judges were evidently undesirable,' James wrote in his diary. 'The thing has been badly handled by all.' Generally prurient press speculation fanned the flames, and eventually the Prime Minister asked the Lord Advocate to investigate the allegations relating to a so-called 'magic circle' of senior Scottish judges. The prominent QC (and future judge) William Nimmo Smith led an exhaustive three-month investigation, which ultimately drew a line under the matter by dismissing the allegations against all those concerned, although the reputational damage to the Scottish justice system would undoubtedly have distressed James.

Later that year, he revived his long-standing interest in music, particularly the piano, perhaps finding it relaxing after the stresses of the previous year. In July, he sat his Grade 8 Pianoforte exam and was delighted to pass 'with distinction', an impressive feat given he had only cleared Grade 5 a few months before. James also stepped up his involvement with various schools and universities, becoming president of the Scottish Universities Law Institute (which oversaw the publication of a series of academic books on Scots Law) in 1991 and taking a day off work to attend Chancellor Helmut Kohl's visit to the Europa Institute and honorary graduation at Edinburgh University ('A charismatic experience,' he wrote in his diary. 'He was on splendid form – a huge man in every way'). James's own position in public life and services to the Law were also recognized when he was granted an honorary doctorate by Heriot-Watt University. James Mackay (who had recommended Clyde for the honour) was installed as Chancellor, and both attended a reception at Edinburgh Art College. 'The day', James reflected in his diary, had been 'a kind of unreal dream'.

Napier granted James a similar honour at Edinburgh's Usher

Hall a few years later, recognition that he had played a central role (as a governor) in its transition from a polytechnic to a university in 1992. Ian J. Miller, at that time Napier's secretary, turned to him for assistance, 'and we sat down with a blank sheet of paper and very quickly (thanks to his skills) produced a document which became the statutory instrument establishing Napier University'. Indeed, it became the model for other emerging universities in Scotland. 'I will not forget his skill as a draughtsman,' reflected Miller in 2009, 'coupled with his charm and enthusiasm.'

James was also hugely active in the affairs of the University of Edinburgh, having succeeded his friend Kenny Cameron in July 1989 as Chancellor's Assessor on the Court, of which he was vice chairman for three years. Lord (Stewart) Sutherland recalled the Queen asking what James did during one visit to the university, to which he replied jokingly that James's job was to keep 'him' – gesticulating in Philip's direction – 'in check', Prince Philip being the Chancellor of the university.

He also found space in an obviously busy life to devote attention to several independent schools in his home city of Edinburgh, continuing a long-standing tradition of judicial involvement in education James cared deeply about students, their aspirations and their difficulties, and also understood the importance of relations with parents, later combining these two concerns as an early trustee of St Mary's Music School in Edinburgh, lending support to what at first appeared an uncertain venture.

James made a particular impression as Chairman of the Council of St George's School for Girls, where he helped recruit its formidable headmistress Judith McClure, who had hitherto perceived judges as 'awesome and remote figures, enveloped in robes and surrounded by ritual'. Gradually, however, he revealed what she called his 'essential humanity'. 'He took Roger and me around Edinburgh, dressed in a cardigan and clutching a bleeper, as he was the judge on call,' she remembered at his memorial service. 'He recommended to me at once the works of his beloved Sir Walter Scott, suggesting I start with *The Heart of Midlothian.*'

Traditionally, a judge chaired the Council of St George's and James followed in a long line of eminent Scottish legal figures. Anne Smith, who also served on the Council, remembered James taking his role 'very seriously'.

> At that time, the Assisted Places Scheme had come to an end and [economic] recessions had also had an impact on school rolls. So, we had to be more creative in terms of facilities, and I remember James saying you can't force the market in girls' schools but as long as there's a demand we must provide the best-quality education possible. His view was that if numbers continued to decline then it would just come to an end, but that didn't happen.

'He was involved in everything,' recalled Judith McClure, 'and it was done in a positive collaborative way.' She continued:

> He gave everyone a chance to develop, and in return every member of the staff at St George's took to him and had a high regard for him. He wanted everyone to play a part, it was just so obvious and so attractive to see, and James treated everyone as an equal. He was a good organiser of meetings, a good organiser of human beings. He would have drinks parties for all the staff. He was careful to build a fun element into hard work.

Even after James stood down as Chairman of the Council he was diligent in remaining involved with what was happening at the school. He continued to serve on its Futures Committee, while the Clyde Award was given to a student who exemplified his approach. He and Ann also funded the landscaping of a vacant area between two parts of the school to create a woodland garden. Because of the steepness of the slope, it became known as 'Clydebank', which Judith McClure called 'a living and growing tribute to them both'.

At James's memorial service, McClure would later quote his own words, 'there is more in life than the law', as characterising his commitment to the service of society throughout his life. 'What he contributed to other people and organisations, particularly those devoted to learning and education,' she said, 'was far more than simply filling the interstices of his formidable career as lawyer and judge.'

The Law might not have been everything, but it continued to form the bedrock of James's life and career. On 27 February 1991, nine children were taken from South Ronaldsay 'to a place of safety' following allegations by social workers of child abuse, and although they were reunited with their parents after five weeks in care on the mainland, the events led to a huge public outcry, and Orkney was awash with rumour and speculation. The Government promised a judicial inquiry and on 5 June, Ian Lang, the Secretary of State for Scotland, wrote asking James to chair it. 'Your appointment would both make it clear to the public the importance which we attach to the matters at issue and guarantee an authoritative investigation of them,' reasoned Lang.

James accepted and was then temporarily 'released' from his work at the Court of Session to conduct an inquiry that would take up more than a year of his life. There was a family precedent of sorts: in April 1945, his father had been appointed to chair a committee of investigation into the state of childcare in Scotland, with his recommendations (published more than a year later), 'Homeless Children', immediately christened the 'Clyde Report'. Events in Orkney, however, were considerably more complex and, above all, sensitive.

It also meant he would exist very much in the public eye,

much more so than was the case with his standard judicial work. When the inquiry remit (which would later cause considerable difficulties) was published, James was filmed by television crews at Parliament House 'doing various judicial things like taking off my gown and looking at a book and writing at a desk'. Neither of his sons remember being conscious of their father's work until that moment. 'He generally gave the impression that what he did was boring and not very interesting,' recalled Jamie Clyde. 'But he couldn't keep Orkney quiet because it was all over the papers – he was on the news every night.'

TV cameras and the press were also out in force when James held a preliminary hearing at Kirkwall Town Hall on 3 July, at which he took care to stress he was not conducting 'litigation between opposing parties, but an objective inquiry into what happened'. Afterwards he was photographed outside St Magnus Cathedral, smartly dressed in a three-piece suit, and on hearing that the Edinburgh flight might not depart the following day because of the weather, got his first taste of the logistical challenge that working in the Northern Isles would pose. 'A taxi and a boat to John O'Groats', he recorded in his diary, having requested an 'alternative escape', 'and a police car to Inverness for me to be at the Station Hotel for the night. What a performance!' Once again in his long and varied career, James found himself on the periphery of the British Isles.

A civil servant called George Aitken, who had recently retired from the Scottish Office, was appointed James's clerk, and he formed a particularly close working relationship with his two assessors, Dr Hugh Morton and Anne Black. As Morton later recalled, from the outset, James made it clear the trio would act as 'a team, and that he expected us to play a full part in discussing with him every detail of the evidence laid before him'.

On 26 August, a Government car took James to Edinburgh Airport so he could begin the inquiry in earnest. Mrs Dickson, his 'macer' at the High Court, met him there and they flew up to Kirkwall together. She would become another key member of the team, looking after lunch and drinks throughout the day at the Town Hall. Stories even circulated of the time she had protected James from potentially serious injury by throwing herself on top of a prisoner who had lunged at the Bench after sentencing.

James would stay at the Foveran Hotel a few miles outside Kirkwall, in a fine setting overlooking Scapa Flow, and on day one of the inquiry everything proceeded as expected. 'I made some opening remarks and Donald Macfadyen Q.C., counsel to the inquiry, made an opening speech,' James recorded in his diary, 'Then we adjourned. Quiet and solitary evening at my hotel. I walked along the road to the west for an hour or so, watched television, did some music theory exercises and had a fine dinner.'

A daily routine was quickly established: proceedings would begin at 10am sharp, a break for lunch at 1pm, and then the afternoon session would go on until just before 4pm. A typed copy of the day's proceedings would be ready by 6.30pm, which James, Anne and Hugh would then go through, identifying any matters that required further discussion. Tuesdays were set aside for a working dinner, which usually took place at a small flat rented by Anne in Kirkwall. 'James and Hugh arrived and we ate supper and then discussed any issues of concern as well as setting the world right,' she recalled fondly. 'He and Hugh usually had an argument as to who would wash and who would dry the dishes!' Hugh recalled:

> We could have quite obscure conversations about some aspects of Scottish history, but we never spoke about politics or religion. I think he was a modest man; he never mentioned the fact his father had chaired a similar inquiry in the 1940s, and although I knew he was interested in music and playing the piano he never ever said to me 'I've just passed this exam or I'm doing this'. I took that as modesty. We would talk about music,

certainly, but he clearly didn't want to risk sounding as
if he was gloating about his own ability.

Anne was similarly impressed by this self-effacing quality, but was
also conscious (like Hugh) that James could be 'quite naïve and
other-worldly'. She remembers him telling her at the beginning
of the inquiry that he planned to wear the same tie every day
for the sake of 'continuity', presumably a slightly baffling reference to the television cameras. At Anne's bedsit, meanwhile,
'he would always ask if he could take his jacket off'. A formal
but stylish dresser, his long black coat and hat would mark him
out during lunch-time strolls through Kirkwall's streets. 'One
day as we got back to the Town Hall,' recalls Anne, 'James asked
me why everyone seemed to recognise him! He was never
self-important.'

Hugh also remembered what he called James's 'subversive
streak', as well as a wise appreciation of human nature tempered
by 'an acute sense of the absurd'. He and Anne were by no
means alone in getting swept up in Clyde's world, his appetite
for life and generosity of spirit, his simple tastes (James would
mark the end of each week with a Tunnock's tea cake) and
rather old-fashioned sense of correctness. 'As you would expect,
he never used bad language even when annoyed,' said Hugh. 'He
preferred the simple exclamation "fiddlesticks" – Anne and I
heard that on a number of occasions!' But above all the assessors
liked their boss on both a personal and professional level. 'That's
why we all put so much into it,' reflected Anne more than two
decades later, 'we wanted to do a good job for him.'

Despite the seriousness of the subject matter, the atmosphere
was congenial, with Donald Mackay (later, as Lord Mackay of
Drumadoon, a judge) acting as an unofficial social convenor by
arranging a series of outings for all those involved in the inquiry,
while George Aitken put together a poetical commentary on
proceedings which he called 'The Official ABC of the Inquiry'.
The inquiry itself, as Hugh Morton observed, was 'inevitably

adversarial in nature, and there was much cross-examination of witnesses, some of it quite hostile'. 'Lord Clyde was, as one would expect, scrupulous in his rulings on which questions would be allowed, and which not.' He also made a point of inviting his two assessors to ask their own questions once he had finished examining a witness.

Before too long, however, problems emerged. Towards the end of August 1991, counsel protested about certain reports in that day's newspapers. This concerned how the children involved were referred to (some were being teased at school), James having sanctioned the use of their first name followed by the initial letter of their surnames. 'Irresponsible and sensational reporting does no service to the public', he cautioned, 'and no service to this public inquiry.' This, however, infuriated the newspapers, who believed they had a clear understanding about how proceedings were to be covered. In the *Mail on Sunday*, columnist Iain Walker condemned James for ruling press 'freedom . . . out of court', although others were generally more positive, journalist Sarah Nelson giving the team credit for having 'managed to create an atmosphere at once calm, tolerant, rigorous, and respectful towards everyone'.

Time was also an issue: on 7 October the Secretary of State for Scotland wrote to James 'anxious that the Inquiry should not be unduly prolonged', and asking for his assessment of its likely length. James replied saying March or April the following year (which turned out to be spot on), but then in November, following a visit to South Ronaldsay to look at the four homes of the children's parents, James's team returned to Kirkwall to see an 'appalling' *Daily Record* headline calling on them to 'STOP THIS GRAVY TRAIN!' 'The *Scotsman* and *Glasgow Herald* leaders are more sensible,' he wrote in his diary, 'but I spent a miserable afternoon worrying about progress.'

The controversy stemmed from a deal negotiated by the Dean of the Faculty of Advocates, Alan Johnston QC, for state-financed counsel which turned out to be eye-wateringly expensive. More to the point, it had led to the withdrawal, or threatened withdrawal, of certain key organisations from the inquiry, for example the British Association of Social Workers (which withdrew after paying £70,000 in legal fees), while Orkney Islands Council and Strathclyde Regional Council publicly reviewed their costs of tens of thousands of pounds for every month they were involved.

This was due in part to the inquiry's remit which, as Johnston complained in a letter to *The Times*, compelled it 'to investigate every aspect of the happenings and the general consequences for the handling of such cases', which had led to delays and, therefore, rising costs. In other words, it had little to do with James, but given his – and the inquiry's – high profile, he ended up taking a lot of the flak, mainly from newspapers still smarting from his earlier comments about their coverage. 'Outwardly he is a dapper, mild-mannered, almost gentle man, who has suc-ceeded in putting at ease those giving evidence inside Kirkwall's 108-year-old town hall,' reported the *Sunday Times*. 'Privately, as the week wore on, his emotions must have ranged between rage and despair as key players threatened to pull out, blaming the crippling cost of representation.'

James met Alan Rodger, the Solicitor General, to set out a more structured timetable for proceedings, and also arranged for the parents' counsel to accept a lower fee so that public funds could be spread to other parties, but beyond that there was not much more James could do. 'At least I've tried,' he wrote in his diary with obvious frustration. 'I am to make a statement on Monday . . . I feel immensely tired. It is all a nightmare.' Morale was generally low, but James was fortified by support from his wife Ann and colleagues like William Prosser, and gradually the crisis eased, with the Scottish Office minister Michael Forsyth intervening to ensure that Orkney Islands Council did not, as threatened, pull out.

There were other consolations. James clearly enjoyed his evening walks on the island, which on one occasion included a 'fine display' of the Northern Lights, described in his diary as 'eerie and magical'. He also had time to work on his music, even transferring his electronic keyboard to his hotel room to work on Chopin and Shostakovich. The time to practice and study paid off, and in April 1992 he passed his Grade 8 theory exam, again with distinction.

On 29 January 1992, James celebrated his sixtieth birthday in Kirkwall. 'I am 60. Can't believe it,' he wrote in his diary. 'The inquiry ploughs on.' His assessors arranged a birthday tea party and, once they had finished the afternoon session, 'a splendid cake'. He was also cheered by some celebratory verse from his son Tim:

> Now that your age is sixty,
> remember when you were fifty,
> don't cry, sniff, weep or go numb,
> because the best is yet to come.

A prescient prediction, but in the interim the Orkney Inquiry moved to a close, at least in terms of gathering evidence. 'Queer feeling of shock and sadness and joy,' James recorded in his diary on 25 March. 'End of term feeling and atmosphere.'

> Everyone packing up . . . Dear hotel, my second home. I have got so used to it. The view over Scapa Flow from the dining room, my little room, the peace and quiet, the little noises when the place is empty. It seems the end of an era. But lots of writing yet to be done. A huge quantity of paper to go South and a lot of luggage. I hope by the time I return I will be on top of it all.

Final submissions were to take place two months later, but by then James had already begun writing up 135 days of accumulated evidence while his two assessors looked at preliminary drafts, checked facts and probed further where necessary. Dr Hugh Morton remembered 'marvelling at his ability to relate one bit of information to another', something he attributed to his unostentatious intellect. 'Working away on polishing the report,' James wrote on 20 July. 'Round and round and still corrections . . . My back is sore.'

James also noted that the police were interested in a recent break-in at No. 9 Heriot Row, someone having told the press that it was linked with files stolen from police HQ at Fettes. James was besieged by calls from journalists, while the following week the *Sun* newspaper screamed 'JUDGE HOME RAID WAS "KIDNAP BID"', going on to claim that animal-rights activists were planning to kidnap one of Lord Clyde's sons (Tim was about to start at Durham University).[1] 'All rather mysterious', he wrote in his diary, 'and worrying.' This, together with more music exams and persistent back pain, proved a distraction as the final edition of the Orkney report was completed.

Both James's assessors expressed their admiration for his handling of a difficult exercise. 'You have carried a tremendous burden through the whole Inquiry and you put so much concern and thought into every stage of it,' wrote Anne Black, while Dr Morton said his 'conduct of what by any standard was a most sensitive & difficult exercise was an object lesson in the arts of tact & sensitivity'. 'What could have been a very fraught business,' he added, 'became instead calm & measured under your direction.' And in return, James made clear his gratitude to his two loyal assessors, sending them personal letters and gifts. The report also included fulsome praise. 'I'm still quite overwhelmed by that,' reflected Morton nearly a quarter century later. 'A line maybe, but a whole paragraph acknowledging our work?'

---

1 When Tim turned twenty-one on 1 October 1994, James, the family and friends donned evening dress and flew to a secret location (which turned out to be in Inverurie) for a surprise birthday party.

The Scottish Secretary and Lord Advocate were similarly grateful for James's dedicated work, Ian Lang thanking James for 'such a full and clear report into circumstances which were both difficult and complicated', and Peter Fraser adding that it was 'clear in its criticisms and at the same time positive in its many recommendations'. On 11 September 1992, James dined with Lang and the Prime Minister, John Major, at Bute House in Edinburgh. 'An interesting but brief discussion from the sweet course on the state of the state,' he noted wryly in his diary. 'I made a contribution. We were all photographed. It was an interesting occasion. Major is courteous, shows an apparent respect and interest, and has the swift mind and manner of the accomplished statesman.'

The report, however, was not yet public, eventually being published on 27 October. James took the afternoon to 'refresh' his memory of the proceedings and at 4pm gave a press conference in the Solicitors to the Supreme Court (SSC) Library following formal presentation of his recommendations to the House of Commons by the Secretary of State for Scotland. 'I took questions', he later wrote in his diary, 'and hope I answered them adequately.' He was being typically self-effacing, for the Lord President later wrote praising his 'masterly' handling of the press conference and general handling of an often 'arduous' inquiry. David Hope continued:

> The loneliness of the bench must have seemed particularly acute in the darker months. But the reward of satisfaction of a job supremely well done was there in the end. It has been very nice to read and hear so many good things about you, in which all of us can draw some satisfaction. The confidence which the public should have in the judiciary has, for quite unwarranted reasons, been shaken repeatedly in recent times. It is immensely reassuring, and invigorating, to feel the current moving in the other direction, as the public

observe the skill, dedication and wisdom which you
have been able to bear on such an immense and difficult task.

'Laws to change after Orkney', read the *Scotsman*'s front-page
headline above a large photograph of James. 'THEY ALL FAILED
THE KIDS,' screamed the *Daily Record*, 'Judge slams EVERY-
ONE in Orkney case fiasco,' while the less hyperbolic *Glasgow
Herald* said, more accurately, 'Lord Clyde calls for reform, not
recrimination'.

While his admirably cogent 360-page report recognised that
social workers faced difficult decisions in order to protect children and accepted that all those involved had acted in good
faith, he also directed criticism at some officials, social workers
and the police for having failed to make what he called a 'vital
distinction' between taking an allegation seriously and believing it. 'Not all of the witnesses,' he said drily, 'appreciated it,
nor did those most closely involved, including members of the
RSSPCC (Royal Scottish Society for the Prevention of Cruelty
to Children) staff always respect it.'

The document also included 194 recommendations to prevent a recurrence, including new national guidelines for the
handling of child abuse cases, urgent research into all forms
of child abuse and a better relationship between the agencies
involved. It had expressly never been part of James's remit to
investigate the truth of the allegations of sexual abuse. 'There is
a humane wisdom even in the smallest details,' wrote the psy-
chologist Bani Shorter, who had been given advance sight of
the report. 'Somehow it appears that you have managed to keep
your focus on the welfare of the child without ignoring the
child's place in a family which includes parents and siblings.'

Shorter also used the word 'dignity' to describe James's work
in Orkney, something echoed by Kenny Cameron, who would
later talk of him having drawn 'on all his reserves of tact, powers
of organisation and strength of character' to help defuse an issue

that had 'disturbed and divided a small community'. Importantly, Orkney Islands Council not only accepted his criticisms but later made a 'wholehearted' apology to the parents and agreed an out-of-court settlement in damages for trauma and distress and expenses payable to each child and parent.

When everything had died down, James attended a dinner at the Signet Library organised by some of those involved, and although he never returned to Orkney he did keep in touch with Hugh and Anne, his two assessors, and regularly gave speeches about the inquiry and the handling of child abuse allegations more generally, demonstrating an ongoing commitment to learning the lessons of what had occurred in February 1991. The childcare profession 'calls for qualities of a high order', he said at one gathering, 'not only humanity and humility but a sensitive expertise and a sound common sense', all qualities he had brought to the Orkney Inquiry.

More than a decade later, James would revisit the Orkney Inquiry, criticising as 'tragic' and 'disappointing' the fact that ministers had ignored many of his recommendations, particularly the establishment of a national unit to investigate complex child abuse cases. In 2003, James became a governor of the then new organisation Children in Scotland, clearly still feeling a great responsibility towards the plight of children in care or suffering at the hands of abusive parents.

In his letter praising James's handling of the Orkney Inquiry, the Lord President (David Hope) had referred to him returning to the Valuation Appeal Court and the 'vagaries of the circuits in Glasgow or elsewhere', adding that it would be 'marvellous, from our point of view, to have you back among us!' Indeed, after a holiday in Austria and Italy, James returned to his old routine on the Bench, and a few months later drove to Durham to help Tim settle in at university. 'Several Edinburgh children there,' he noted in his diary. 'Sweetie and I drove back rather sadly to a quiet and empty house.'

In January 1993, James turned sixty-one, but did 'not feel it', perhaps because the experience of chairing a major public inquiry had given him a new lease of professional life, as well as a higher public profile than most of his contemporaries. In September that year, the BBC began filming James for a series of televised trials, an experiment arguably in keeping with his belief that justice should not only be done, but be *seen* to be done. It was the first time television cameras had been allowed into court for a criminal trial, and while the experiment was not repeated, James's quiet control of proceedings was clear from the resulting broadcasts.

It also earned him some fan mail from a fellow Edinburgh Academical, who said how much he had enjoyed the five programmes. 'Now that you have had a chance to view the finished product, I hope you are pleased with the result,' wrote Wing Commander Frank Cattle (Ret'd):

> Another aspect that I found impressive was the aura of authority emanating from the judges; it was partly the character in their faces, partly the brevity and clarity of what they said and partly what they actually did say and how they said it . . . may I offer my congratulations on a thoroughly professional series which showed the courts of Scotland in action warts and all and gave the ordinary viewer, like me, a fascinating insight into justice being done and being seen to be done – right there, in front of your very eyes!

In May 1995, the Lord President appointed James to the Inner House of the Court of Session in succession to Lord Mayfield, who had retired, while a few months later Michael Forsyth, the new Secretary of State for Scotland, asked him to become Chairman of the new Scottish Valuation and Rating Council, which he accepted.

His reputation as a judge remained extremely sound, although that year he was criticised for being too lenient in his sentencing for two separate cases, one in which he gave a man probation after he had bitten off a policeman's ear, and another in which he jailed two thugs for four years after a particularly vicious attack outside a Glasgow nightclub. The latter sentence was later raised to seven years after an unprecedented Crown appeal. Otherwise James, as David Hope had predicted in 1992, remained busy with the 'vagaries' of the 'Glasgow Circuit', which could involve pretty gruelling criminal cases and lengthy stays (in basic accommodation) far from home comforts.

James had just finished an assault and extortion case in Glasgow, followed by a speech day and dinner at St George's, when his 'whole evening was thrown into confusion' by a letter from the Prime Minister offering him appointment as a Lord of Appeal in Ordinary, or Law Lord, a position first linked with the Clyde name back in 1986. Harry (Lord) Keith had finally retired after nearly twenty years, and now James was being asked if he would like to replace him. But his reaction was surprising. 'I had always looked to that as one goal', he confided to his diary, 'but now it has come I am curiously muddled and confused.' Nevertheless, on 5 July James wrote to Downing Street saying he had 'very much pleasure in accepting this proposal'.

Back in Glasgow the following day, James's head was 'in a whirl with emotion', even more so on discovering that David Hope was to be joining him as the other Scottish Law Lord. 'Now I begin to read into a phone call from Alan Johnston [Dean of the Faculty] last week that there might have been a possibility that I could have succeeded David as Lord President,' he reflected in his diary. 'But when he raised it I expressed doubt – really feeling that I was too old and it was too late. What have I done?'

Whatever the case (and it seems unlikely that was Johnston's implication), James, aware it was an odd way to react to a promotion, gradually adjusted to the new situation, reassured by a long talk with his son Jamie. 'There are a lot of rumours flying about,' he noted in his diary on 9 July, the news still having not been made public, 'some of them quite accurate.' Ten days later his and David Hope's appointments were formally announced. The new Lord President, meanwhile, was the former Lord Advocate (and recent appointee to the Bench) Alan Rodger.

Letters of congratulation began to arrive at No. 9 Heriot Row. David Edward said he was 'over the moon' to hear of his friend's 'translation to London', where he said it was time Scotland was 'represented by people with some imagination!' George Emslie (the former Lord President) said his elevation was 'a belated recognition of your outstanding qualities', while Emslie's son Nigel said it was 'hard to believe that a quarter of a century has gone by since I had the great pleasure and privilege of devilling to you. I am so pleased about your elevation to the Lords . . . The Judicial Committee has always needed people of real stature from north of the border.'

Colleagues from south of the border also got in touch. Lord (Leonard) Hoffmann wrote of his delight that James would 'once again be a colleague', having first encountered each other in Jersey and Guernsey. He offered help finding accommodation, and later agreed to act as one of James's sponsors upon his introduction to the House of Lords.

On 3 September 1996, James travelled to London to look at flats in the Victoria area close to Parliament, and also saw the Garter Principal King of Arms in the afternoon, 'the object of the trip', as he noted in his diary, 'and settled my new title'. This, as *The Times*' Court Circular announced on 4 October, was a life barony 'by the style of Baron Clyde, of Briglands in Perthshire and Kinross'. As Nigel Emslie had observed in a letter to James a few months before, the 'great judicial tradition' of the Clyde family was 'now appropriately continued'.

Chapter 8

The Other Scottish Judge

When James matriculated his coat of arms as a new peer, he chose to represent his enthusiasms and personal philosophy in a crest containing a branch of mountain ash, beech and cherry supporting the figure of justice holding scales (but without a blindfold) and the figure of Apollo with a lyre, together with the motto *Diligens Integer Laetus* ('Hard-working, honourable, happy').

He had always taken considerable care over his Latin, and those words were well chosen: since joining the Bar back in 1959 James had maintained a punishing schedule of legal and voluntary work, conscientiously abiding by the highest possible standards of integrity and compassion, and despite several setbacks over the years he had always remained cheerful in adversity: as one colleague put it, a 'happy warrior'.

Friends had played a part in the appointment, with both David Hope (the outgoing Lord President) and James Mackay (the Lord Chancellor) having long considered him top of their list should a vacancy arise on the appellate committee of the House of Lords. And now it had, James was to transfer all his professional and personal qualities from Parliament House in Edinburgh to the British Parliament at Westminster.

The Times' profile of the new Law Lord observed that he held 'liberal views on law reform' and was even 'considered a

radical in many circles'. Given that the House of Lords had no
jurisdiction in criminal cases emanating from Scotland, James's
expertise in civil law was especially useful, as was his grasp of
the European dimension when the European Convention on
Human Rights was incorporated into UK Law.

There were usually about a dozen Lords of Appeal in Ordinary
at any one time, including two Scots and one specifically covering Northern Ireland, and the atmosphere in their offices in
the Upper House was clubbable. James, therefore, fitted in well,
what James Mackay called his 'infectious laugh' echoing around
the corridor. 'The House of Lords was such a relaxation after
Edinburgh,' recalled David Hope, who also became a Law Lord
in 1996, 'there was much more time to think, to reflect and to
enjoy life, and I think James loved it for that reason.'

It also meant that ambitions (and associated worries) that had
dogged him since the 1970s now receded. The Lord Presidency
was no longer a realisable goal, and in any case James had now
overtaken his father and grandfather to become a Law Lord, a
more senior (and UK-wide) judicial appointment. This enabled
him to do interesting and important work, of relevance not just
to the UK but also to Europe and the wider Commonwealth
via (the Judicial Committee of) the Privy Council, of which he
also became a member.

On 15 October 1996 James reported to the Privy Council
Office on Whitehall for a briefing and a rehearsal, and was
then driven to Buckingham Palace for the ceremony itself. He
slipped up slightly, saying 'good morning, ma'am' rather than
'good morning, Your Majesty' as instructed, but he then kneeled
('rather clumsily') and kissed the Sovereign's hand before taking
another oath. Back at the House of Lords, he had lunch with
Ann before locating his rooms and 'a pile of papers'.

The following day there was another ceremony, this time
James's introduction to the House of Lords. After another lunch
with Ann, this time joined by Jamie, Tim, Black Rod and friends
like the Lords Woolf and Hoffmann (both fellow Law Lords), he

and his supporters 'were taken away to be robed, photographed and drilled'. 'Then the House sat and we paraded in, bowing here and there . . . and reading an oath,' as he later wrote in his diary, 'signing a parchment and then sitting and standing and bowing three times in unison before parading out.' Watching was Lord Hope, who along with the other Lords of Appeal had taken time off from a case to attend. As Hope recalled in his own diary:

> James chose Harry Woolf and Lennie Hoffmann to be his supporters, a nice choice but interesting also that he was clearly not inclined to follow the Scottish tradition of asking, as I did in my case, Scots Law Lords to fulfil this function. There is a strong independent streak in his make-up. He plans to travel by rail. I go by air. He wants to live out of the Inns, while I am still hopeful that Gray's Inn will give me a place in which to live. He took the oath of allegiance in a very loud, firm voice and looked very fine indeed.

Later that day James returned to the Upper House, where he spotted his two sons in the gallery, and the following day dealt with his first appeal. 'I spent the afternoon writing and dictating an opinion,' he wrote contentedly. 'Lunch with the Law Lords, jolly. Everyone is so terribly kind.'

It was not until December, however, that James learned of an opportunity to make his maiden speech, albeit during a debate on the Human Embryology Act. But he hastily readjusted his travel plans (he had been due to fly back to Scotland) and 'decided to plunge in':

> The debate began before 5.0. I was fifth in line and felt rather dry mouthed but it went all right. People are traditionally congratulatory but I hope they meant it. Viscount Simon of Glaisdale staggered up the steps to

me and said in a loud aside (which as he is deaf could
be heard throughout the Chamber) 'Your father would
be very proud of you.' I smiled a thank you, fearing the
incident had been heard by all.

James then dined at the House and walked back to the
Lansdowne Club (a temporary residence while he found a flat
nearer Westminster) 'on air'. 'I do feel at last', he told his diary,
'that I have arrived.'

The following month he celebrated his sixty-fifth birthday. 'An Old Age Pensioner,' he noted in his diary. 'No more
National Insurance deducted from my pay. And a little pension
too!' Further honours came his way. His old Oxford college,
Corpus Christi, made him an Honorary Fellow (which included
the right, as the president wrote to inform him, 'to free lunch
and dinner, but not drinks!'), while on 6 February 1997 he
was elected to the Bench of the Middle Temple as an honorary
member, as had his father back in 1958, a sign that his expertise
was also valued by the English legal profession.

But, as ever, judicial promotion meant giving up other activities,
in James's case his role as Chancellor's Assessor at the University
of Edinburgh. The Duke of Edinburgh wrote to express his
sadness on 29 September 1996 and also initiated a dinner at
Old College to mark James's 'retirement' on 19 February the
following year. And having spent that day in London, James was
even offered a lift north on the royal plane, making his way to
RAF Northolt where he boarded a jet aircraft equipped with
passenger compartments. As he recorded in his diary:

> I was told the single chair facing to the rear at the other
> side of the passage was for the Duke of Edinburgh.
> A man came and put a jacket on it. Then we turned
> round to take off and I realised that the Duke was the
> pilot! I had been offered a lift to Edinburgh on the royal

plane for the dinner at the University but I had not guessed that HRH would drive it. The weather was awful. Squalls of rain and gusty winds. But he lifted the plane with few bumps and jolts to 26,000 feet when all was calm. Then he came to join us.

They had tea and cakes, chatted about flying and the day's events, then Prince Philip got up and returned to the cockpit, 'taking the plane down from 26,000 feet to a superb landing at Turnhouse, despite a gusting sidewind. I gathered that pilots genuinely admire his skill in handling a plane.'

At the dinner itself, held in the sumptuous surroundings of the Playfair Library, James and Ann flanked the Duke of Edinburgh, who made a speech and presented his former assessor with a silver quaich. 'I made a reasonable speech in reply – no notes and then funny stories, one a little risqué,' he reflected in his diary. 'But HRH enjoyed it. Then coffee and departures. What an extraordinary day.' A few months later, the University once again expressed its gratitude by awarding James an honorary doctorate.

In March 1997, James and Ann also said farewell to No. 9 Heriot Row. 'Hard to believe we are out, after over 20 years,' he reflected in his diary. 'And out of Heriot Row after over 65 years! So sad to see the empty house, but what a vast pile it is. And now we are in to No. 12 Dublin Street, and order emerges out of chaos.' Their original plan had been to retire to a mews flat they had bought in 1988, but instead discovered, as James later wrote, 'the joy of a house which faced east and west rather than north and south', having made arrangements to leave Heriot Row altogether shortly before his appointment as a Law Lord. At Dublin Street, he and Ann would later create a beautifully laid out garden (much like that at Shiel), while in London James took a flat at Westminster Mansions on Great Smith Street, which became affectionately known as 'the cupboard'.

Parliament in general and the Upper House in particular were about to undergo considerable change following the landslide election of a Labour government in May 1997. 'No Scottish MP's for the Conservatives!' wrote James, having stayed up to watch some of the results come in. 'T[ony] Blair is Prime Minister. We feel sorry for those like Malcolm Rifkind who have lost out.' And two weeks later, he and Ann attended the State Opening of Parliament. 'I robed and Sweetie like all the ladies in evening dress, with tiara (borrowed) and the family diamonds. Looked superb. A splendid occasion. Then a drinks party at the Lord Chancellor's.'

Another consequence of the election was that devolution for Scotland, which James had supported since standing for Parliament in 1974, was now to become a reality. He participated in the Committee stages of the resulting Scotland Bill, which in 1999 would provide the legislative basis for the Scottish Parliament in Edinburgh, while in 1998 he was appointed Chairman of Parliament's Joint Committee on Consolidation Bills.

On the Appellate Committee, meanwhile, James quickly came to be seen as a fine judge, of independent mind and able to make a contribution to the Law of England as well as his native Scotland. At the same time, he was prepared to question the reason for differences between the two systems. In *Smith v. Bank of Scotland* (1997), for example, he delivered the leading judgement bringing the principles on caution in Scots Law into line with those governing surety in England. An incisive intellect also compelled him to justify legal concepts. In *Banque Financière de la Cité v. Parc (Battersea) Ltd and Others* (1998) James analysed the principle of unjust enrichment as one more fully expressed in the Latin formulation *nemo debet locupletari ex aliena iactura* ('no one should be enriched by another's loss'). In *Royal Bank of Scotland v. Etridge No. 2* (2001), he questioned the value of a distinction between actual and presumed undue influence.

James's experience as a prosecutor also proved valuable when the Privy Council considered issues relating to Scottish criminal law, one particularly influential judgement being *McLean v. Buchanan* (2001) concerning criminal legal aid regulations in Scotland, in which he observed that: 'The requirements of fairness in judicial proceedings are rarely, if ever, met by blanket measures of universal application. Universal policies which make no allowance for exceptional cases will not readily meet the standards required for fairness and justice.'

Although James did not serve as a Law Lord for nearly as long as many others, not least his predecessor Harry Keith's nearly two decades, within a few years he had sat on more appeals than any of his colleagues and contributed ably to the judicial work he undertook, providing judgements which remained important and intellectually impressive decades later. 'He enjoyed most the argument, the intellectual engagement of being a Law Lord,' reflected Anne Smith. 'He wrote well, his judgements were very good; he had a great talent for making complex law appear very straightforward.' Many of his judgements displayed strong empathy and humanity, especially any cases involving children.

Lord Hoffmann, who served alongside James having first encountered him in the Channel Islands in the early 1980s, remembered Clyde clearly 'thinking for himself but never putting himself forward in the way some people – including myself – in terms of persuading others of his view'. He continued:

> James would never try to twist my arm on cases, if he hadn't managed to convince me in writing then it wouldn't happen in person. He was too modest for that sort of thing. I think he may have been more inclined as to the merits of a case than I was. I was keener on hard-edged rules, whereas James was more inclined to make the rules more flexible to fit with what he thought the right outcome should be. I remember one case in which we split 3/2 over a tenant who wanted the council to fit a wash basin in her loo; she said not having one was a danger to her health, her kids weren't washing their hands and then touching food, etc. She quoted an Act which I think related to a cholera epidemic, so her

situation clearly wasn't what the legislation had in mind. I said no, it would set an expensive precedent, not our concern as judges, etc, but James and another colleague took the view that she ought to have a basin because it was the right thing to do. I was on the winning side of that case, but it revealed something of James's approach: to get to justice between the two parties.

Newspaper profiles frequently noted James's quiet, meticulous style, 'industrious and pleasant with a human touch', just as it had been at the Bar, on the Bench and during the Orkney Inquiry. Sometimes he was referred to as 'the other Scottish judge', an indication that David Hope – despite being a few years younger – was considered the more senior given his service as Lord President and Lord Justice Clerk. In 1998 and 1999, meanwhile, James undertook with Denis Edwards the preparation and publication of the first systematic account of judicial review in Scots Law, *Judicial Review* (2000), which one reviewer described as 'an extremely scholarly and admirably timely book' when it appeared at the end of 1999.

'When I was small I wondered if I would live to see the next century,' wrote James in his diary on 1 January 2000. 'And here we are.' As usual he and Ann headed up to Shiel, although it proved too windy to make use of 'a very expensive' firework. The highlight of millennium year was a trip to Malaysia, to which he flew immediately after an appeal case involving Imperial Tobacco, which meant he received several long-distance calls from colleagues trying to persuade him to decide one way or the other due to a split bench.

In Malaysia, he and Ann found the church where her parents had married in 1932 (and she had been christened), the chaplain even managing to locate the original wedding banns.[1]

---

1   The church had been bombed in the war and many of its archives lost. Fortunately, the wedding banns had somehow been saved.

At the Penang Sports Club, they also met an 'ancient man' who remembered Ann's father as 'the most brilliant cricketer'. Sadly, they were too late to see Ann's childhood home, which had become a building site. There was work to do too, James being entertained by the Bar Council in Penang and meeting some High Court judges.

Upon his return to the UK (always a traditional dresser, he picked up a new tailor-made suit en route to the airport), James's thoughts appear to have turned to retirement. He had endured various health problems over the past couple of years, including a lump on his neck, and at one point even visited a healer in West Dulwich in hope of some respite. One of the healer's predictions was that James would retire at the end of 1999 but, in the event, he informed the Lord Chancellor, Derry Irvine, of his intention on 24 April 2001, effective as of 30 September. 'Feel rather miserable,' he confessed to his diary. 'Haven't told anyone else.'

Colleagues were surprised – judges were compelled to retire at seventy-five, which gave James another six years – but understood that even the logistics of travelling down from Edinburgh every Sunday afternoon and back on Thursday evening had been taking their toll. Towards the end of July, Ann helped him clear out his office at the House of Lords, before dining with David Hope and attending a farewell party with a few clerks. James also hosted an 'At Home' drinks party at the Lansdowne Club for about fifty-five colleagues and friends. 'Some think I am retiring prematurely,' he later wrote in his diary. 'Blow that!'

Chapter 9

Justice Oversight Commissioner

James's retirement as a Law Lord was effective as of 1 October 2001, when he was succeeded by the outgoing Lord President, Alan Rodger. Writing to thank him for his five years' service in the House of Lords, the Lord Chancellor, Derry Irvine, drew out two major aspects of his work, 'the first substantive and the second personal':

> You have sat on all the Scottish devolution issue cases and given judgments in very many of them. Your contribution in this area has been particularly notable and, from a judicial standpoint, the transition to devolution and its bedding down has been well managed. More personally, apart from your great expedition as a Law Lord, I know how collegiate all the other Law Lords have found you and how very sorry they will be to see you go.

James replied to say it was 'pleasant to be able to look forward to the occasional possibility of helping out in the future', and that he proposed to retain his London pied-à-terre – otherwise known as 'the cupboard' – in the meantime.

And with Tony Blair's second Labour government keen to transfer the judicial functions of the Upper House to a new

Supreme Court, he hoped that nothing would disturb its 'collegiate' nature. 'I have come to value particularly the co-operation, support, tolerance and goodwill which a group of its size can develop and which makes the work and the company so very congenial,' wrote James. 'It all contributes to making the work a pleasure as well as a privilege.'

Unfortunately for James, the day of his retirement also brought the news he had been diagnosed with non-Hodgkin lymphoma (a cancer affecting the immune system), resulting in an operation that left him 'weak and shocked'. Typically, his illness did not diminish his sense of humour, although he found the treatment 'tedious and wearisome', as he described it in a letter to his old friend and colleague Kenny Cameron in November 2001. He recovered sufficiently to undergo four cycles of chemotherapy in early 2002, and although he was able to start work on a criminal appeal in the Upper House on 29 January (also his seventieth birthday), he was not properly on his feet again until that summer.

In the House of Lords, James now sat as a crossbencher (non-party aligned) rather than a Law Lord, and helped out, given he was still below the statutory retirement age, with occasional judicial business and Privy Council work, with colleagues (both Scottish and English) delighted to hear his distinctive, infectious laugh echo along the corridor he knew so well. One such case required James and four other judges to decide whether a Jamaican national from Kingston ought to receive the death sentence, one of the only times his son Jamie witnessed his father in a professional context.

In *Millar v. Dickson* (2002), James had dealt with a case (before his retirement) concerning the right under the European Convention on Human Rights to a trial before an independent and impartial tribunal, a Scottish devolution case about the use of temporary sheriffs as trial judges. He referred to the fundamental constitutional importance of judicial independence while warning that the principle was not so robust that it could always withstand the pressure that some forms of government might impose upon it, an echo of his original Latin thesis ('we should resist to our last breath those who seek to enslave us') on joining the Bar more than forty years earlier.

In September 2002, James and Ann attended Jamie's wedding, watching with pride as he and Tim made speeches, 'the former sincere and moving, and the latter witty and amusing. Enormously impressive. They are wonderfully gifted, seeming at ease and in control, speaking with authority.' At the end of 2003, the Clydes celebrated the arrival of a grandson ('Jamie sent a picture by email'), another James, the seventh first-born in the family with that name, although he would later become known as 'Moog' to avoid confusion. Earlier that year, James and Ann had held an afternoon tea party at the Savoy Hotel in London to celebrate their ruby wedding anniversary (they had been married in August 1963). 'About 70 guests and 8 children from 3.0 to 6.0.,' he wrote in his diary. 'It all went pretty well . . . I have the new signet ring which [Ann] has given me – 40 years on.' It was also a very hot party; the hotel's air conditioning having failed in 32-degree temperatures.

As James's reaction to the belief in some quarters that he was somehow stepping back from public life having retired as a Law Lord ('Blow that!') suggested, he still felt he had something to contribute in legal terms. And having worked in Scotland, the Channel Islands and most recently England, he now set his sights on another jurisdiction – once again at the periphery of the British Isles – Northern Ireland.

The Belfast Agreement of April 1998 had, as part of a cross-party and inter-governmental plan to bring peace to Northern Ireland after decades of sectarian strife, promised a wide-ranging review of policing and criminal justice in the Province. In March 2000, the Criminal Justice Review Group published 294 recommendations for reform, and in November 2001 the Government published a draft Bill that became the Justice

(Northern Ireland) Act 2002. Every step in this process had been controversial, and its ultimate success depended upon full and effective implementation.

In December 2002, Peter Hain, the Secretary of State for Northern Ireland, announced his intention to appoint a Justice Oversight Commissioner to monitor implementation of nearly 300 changes. This was to be a person of standing who was expected to help create a system of criminal justice that enjoyed the confidence of all parts of the community, Protestant and Catholic. James offered himself for selection and, following an open competition, was appointed.

In applying for the three-year (but part-time) post, James hoped it would aid his recovery and also be 'fun' (i.e. intellectually stimulating). Despite a degree of apprehension at the beginning, it proved to be work for which he was ideally suited. Not only did he have, as the job spec had required, 'standing', but also, as had proved so useful during the Orkney Inquiry, tact and humanity. Anyone attempting to navigate judicial (and indeed political) terrain as complicated as Northern Ireland's needed lots of that, not to mention charm and endless patience.

James began his work on 18 June 2003, giving considerable thought at the outset to getting to grips with the scale and extent of the role and its demands, the sheer range of bodies (and parties) he would be required to deal with and the relationships involved. Of course, he had help. In an echo of the close-knit and loyal team he had gathered around him in Kirkwall a decade before, a carefully chosen team of research consultants was recruited from Scotland, as well as three members of staff based in Belfast.

Sheriff Frank Crowe, one of the 'research consultants', still has letters wooing him in the autumn of 2003. In one, James refers to his post as 'something of an after-thought' which had 'been dropped in to a process which is well begun, although perhaps not half done'. His first report was due in December, which left very little time. 'The task' between then and now, explained James, 'will basically be one of clearing up obscurities and uncertainties' and he hoped Crowe would be able to take 'part in what should not be a very onerous, but in the public perception is an important, part in this interesting development for Northern Ireland'. In another note, which revealed James's irreverence, he added: 'I hope the Powers That Be will release you. This letter is written in the optimistic view that they will.'

The powers that be did release Crowe, and also another research consultant called Gail Patrick, later a sheriff, who had first encountered James as a witness at the Orkney Inquiry (Frank, on the other hand, had a background in forensic medicine). James was required to report to the Secretary of State for Northern Ireland, Lord Chancellor and Attorney General for England and Wales every six months, which indicated how seriously the Government took one of the last elements of the historic Good Friday Agreement. His diary from August 2003 gives a taste of what was involved:

4 August

A long day of meetings with the political parties in Stormont – the SDLP, Sinn Fein, DUP, Alliance, Women's Coalition and PUP. A little wearing and I don't know how it went. I was alone as it was thought inappropriate to have my helper (John Todd this week) from the Criminal Justice Department with me. A spectrum of views and attitudes but mostly in their own ways supportive.

5 August

In the evening dinner at Hillsborough Castle with the Secretary of State and others. Good dinner and an amazing setting. Travelled there with a fearsome display of lightning. Hope I presented myself well enough.

7 August

A meeting with the police – six of them at their HQ.
Quite productive. Back to Stormont for lunch and
then a visit to . . . the Police Oversight Commissioner's
office – interesting to hear of their methods and
facilities.

On 13 October, James went for a check-up at the Western
General and was deemed to be 'fit and well' before returning to
Belfast for a lecture at Queen's University on life imprisonment.
'Spoke with useful people afterwards,' he noted in his diary, 'put
my foot in it with a reckless use of language. Must be more
diplomatic.' Although naturally careful with his language, even
he was finding Northern Ireland a bit of a minefield, despite
having received a lengthy briefing document the week before
setting out 'acceptable' terms and unacceptable 'jargon'.

In the middle of December, James published his First Report
(out of a total of six), followed by a press conference and media
interviews. He concluded that Northern Ireland was on course
for a modern criminal justice system that would speed up the
passage of court cases while protecting victims and witnesses,
but warned that the absence of a functioning devolved government at Stormont (it had been suspended in 2002) was holding
up a number of significant reforms.

Nevertheless, he said there had been 'significant' and 'impressive' progress in overhauling the Province's judicial system, and
a 'solid start' made on implementing nearly 300 recommendations. James also said more needed to be done to address the
'historically low' number of Catholics employed in the Northern
Ireland Office's criminal justice department, while highlight-
ing that the prison service similarly remained predominantly
Protestant and male. There was some criticism. Sinn Fein raised
the issue of emblems (i.e. the coat of arms of the British Crown)
in court buildings and questioned whether James would have

enough time to ensure that every last recommendation was put in place.

There were also some mishaps. At the end of 2003, James left some papers relating to his work on top of a hotplate in his library at Dublin Street. This turned itself on due to a fault, badly burning the documents but being discovered before it could spread. Although most were of no importance, he lost some useful notes and files and, as ever, fretted over the public consequences that might have arisen had more substantial documents been involved. And, less seriously, in unveiling his Second Report the following year, he reached the podium to find that the pages of his speech 'were all out of order'. 'I hoped it was not too obvious that I had to rearrange them as I went along,' he later recorded in his diary. There followed more TV and radio interviews, which James generally found a bit of a chore.

In one magazine interview, he explained the 'somewhat elaborate' method he had adopted to record progress of implementation for each of the 294 recommendations:

> This charts the steps through four stages to take account of how far work has gone on each and how far I and my team are satisfied that the work has in fact been carried through to an effective result. So the table which has formed the final appendix to each of my past reports may give some useful measure of progress.

James also stressed what he was *not* required to do. 'It is not part of my remit as Oversight Commissioner', he pointed out several times, 'to advise how things ought or ought not to be done.' But he had been conscious from the start about the 'prime importance' of achieving justice for both victims and offenders as swiftly as possible. Asked about his ambition for the criminal justice system in Northern Ireland, he replied, simply but effectively: 'To secure a system of criminal justice in which all the people of Northern Ireland may have a real pride and which may serve as a model for other countries.'

Like many others who had worked with James over the years, Frank Crowe noticed (and came to admire) some of his essential characteristics. 'He could come over as an aristocratic establishment figure,' he recalled,

> but his personal charm was such that he was seen as someone with whom everyone could work and make good progress. James was very disarming and would listen; it was obvious to everyone he was a fair man, incredibly hard working and clearly doing his best. As Justice Oversight Commissioner, he was very adept at maintaining a public face, meeting people and making public statements. He was also a great team leader and team player.

James disliked flashy hotels, finding modest establishments like Belfast's Holiday Inn more to his taste, while Crowe (a Roman Catholic) reckoned Lord Clyde's Episcopalian beliefs were an asset in that he usefully straddled Northern Ireland's Catholic–Protestant divide. And, of course, there was what the Very Revd Dr Graham Forbes recalled as James's 'very warm, very infectious laughter'. 'I remember being on a Flybe flight to Belfast from Edinburgh,' he said, 'and there was no need to announce his presence on the plane, I could hear him!'

At the beginning of 2005, James launched his Third Report, followed by the usual interviews and a party at his office. In another minor mishap, he accidentally allowed Sir Reg Empey (of the Ulster Unionist Party, or UUP) to take away a copy of his Fourth Report after a hastily arranged meeting at Belfast Airport, which, as the report was still under embargo, caused a bit of concern. Much to his surprise, he found himself getting along better with Nationalists than Unionists, at one meeting finding Sinn Fein 'as agreeable and seeming charming as ever', later noting with approval that their representatives were 'looking more smart, tidy and civilised than when I first met them'. But then, as he was careful to observe in his diary, it was generally 'hard to know how sincere' everyone was given the sensitivities involved.

James noted in his diary on 17 January:

> Meetings with Lady Hermon [UUP] at the Culloden Hotel, with the Alliance Party in University Street and with the SDLP in their office. The [last] was rigorous and depressing. I felt I was making inadequate replies and left a bit shaken. John [Home] was fairly silent and I wish I knew if he disliked my performance. The big subject is community restorative justice and the SDLP has very strong views on the dangers of it developing as a republican project, giving political strength to Sinn Fein. Oh dear. I do find it wearisome and depressing.

Nevertheless, two days later James's Fifth Report appeared ('I made one unfortunate remark to the press which they have picked up,' he recorded in his diary, 'not very serious but just annoying'), and then the Sixth (and final) Report began to take shape. He regularly saw ministers to keep them updated with progress and problems, sometimes at Westminster if he happened to be involved with Privy Council or House of Lords cases (he had sat nine or ten times following his retirement). By May 2006 everything, as James noted in his diary, was 'moving to the close'.

Peter Hain, the Northern Irish Secretary, was the first to see the fruits of James's labours at the end of that month, and wrote at length to say how 'immensely grateful' he was for 'the hard work and dedication you have shown, not only in producing such a detailed and thoughtful report, but also in your whole oversight task'. Hain continued:

I know that it has been done with the support of a very fine team, and in cooperation with officials from across the system. But I am certain that without your engagement, direction, consideration and expertise we would not now be looking at such a valuable end result. Moreover, I consider that the pace of progress can in large part be attributed to the awareness of your constant scrutiny that has permeated the criminal justice community! You have made an invaluable contribution to the Government's efforts to fulfil its commitments under the Belfast Agreement.

Criminal justice was naturally less headline-grabbing than other aspects of the historic Belfast Agreement, but undeniably important, and the Lord Chancellor similarly praised work he deemed 'of the highest quality'.

On 15 June 2006, James published his Sixth Report, announcing that while some of the original 294 recommendations still awaited the restoration of devolution, otherwise some twelve remained outstanding. He was also careful to stress that publication of that report was not the end of the process. Brian Rowntree, chairman of Northern Ireland's Probation Board, praised his 'honest and balanced commentary on what has been the single biggest reform of criminal justice in the western world for at least 40 years'. 'We in Northern Ireland owe you a huge debt of gratitude for the fully inclusive approach taken by you in your transparent reporting,' he added. 'The foundations have been laid, and as you quite rightly reflected in your speech, we now need to action at all levels the recommendations set forth.'

The next day Ann flew over from Edinburgh to join James in his final farewells to his staff followed by a 'very jolly' lunch. Afterwards Gail Patrick, who together with Frank Crowe had become close to James over the past three years, said it had been 'a unique and enjoyable time for us consultants'. 'We are, however, conscious that we only contributed to the tip of the iceberg,'

she added. 'You had the huge responsibility for everything and
the additional stress of meeting endless deadlines. Frank and I
were delighted to be at the final launch and it was clear then, as
throughout, what a brilliant job you did.'

Later they visited the Giant's Causeway ('moderately impressive') then prepared to leave: 'an official car for the last time to
the airport. And so home. Unpacked and started re-orientating.'
James was, however, scheduled to visit Belfast one last time on
15 August, so that judges in Northern Ireland could mark their
appreciation with some 'modest hospitality', in other words a
formal dinner in the memorable surroundings of Hillsborough
Castle.

'Odd again to be back there,' James reflected in his diary:

> The driver met me . . . as arranged and took me to
> Hillsborough Castle where I was dined by the Minister
> of State David Hanson MP and members of the
> Criminal Justice Board. All somehow unreal. It all
> seems so long ago. I did not feel myself but I think
> it all passed all right. I am staying in the 'maisonette'
> attached to the Castle – a pleasant little suite and quiet.

James had welcomed the opportunity to say a final farewell to
members of the Criminal Justice Board, 'whose efforts I have so
much admired over the past three years'. As he added in a letter
to David Hanson:

> Having achieved such a remarkable process of reform
> in such a relatively short period I do hope that the
> energy which the agencies have demonstrated in the
> past will continue towards a greater and greater effi-
> ciency in the operation of the system. I am sure that
> there is a real potential for a model system in Northern
> Ireland in which everyone despite other differences can
> take pride. Perhaps in time the merits of it all will come

to be recognised. It is sad that the media and the public seem more concerned with criticism than with praise.

In spite of that final sentence, James had clearly enjoyed his three years as Justice Oversight Commissioner, and indeed friends and colleagues later came to regard it as perhaps his most important contribution to public life. He had found meeting so many different people stimulating, and particularly loved the Irish sense of humour.

Shortly after delivering his final report in Belfast, James attended a reunion of Edinburgh Academicals who had left the school before 1958 (he had left in 1951). 'Many old acquaintances and friends,' he later wrote in his diary. 'Saw round the school . . . A reception and then dinner. Some pleasant chat. People remembered my appearances in Gilbert & Sullivan.'

At this stage in James's life there were many reminders of his long career. At the end of 2002, George (Lord) Emslie had passed away, a great admirer who had directed his son Nigel towards him as a devil-master, and later spoke of James as his successor as Lord President. In May 2006, he and Ann had also attended a dinner at Holyrood Palace with that year's Lord High Commissioner to the General Assembly of the Church of Scotland, James Mackay. 'He is very gracious and dignified but as always himself, kind and courteous,' James noted in his diary with a touch of melancholy. 'A good dinner with some old friends and some new . . . A curious re-gathering of old acquaintances which I find sad and disturbing.'

As of 2004, James had served as Chairman of the Faculty of Advocates Disciplinary Tribunal, but as of 2007 he reached the statutory judicial retirement age and stepped down, according to statute being 'no longer capable of judicial work'. He turned seventy-five on 29 January but could not quite believe it. 'Am I really that old?' he asked his diary rhetorically. 'I still feel pretty well. A bit wheezy on the steeper streets but still fairly mobile.

Long may it remain so.' Gradually he decluttered, giving away a large quantity of his old law books in the process.

Public life also kept him busy; he involved himself with Lord (David) Steel's modest proposals for reform of the House of Lords and attended the installation of the new Chancellor of Napier University, Tim Waterstone, in November 2007. 'We all robed in the Surgeon's College and processed across the road [to the Festival Theatre],' he noted in his diary, 'traffic stopped and all very colourful.' He also worked on a second edition of his well-received book with Denis Edwards, *Judicial Review* ('something to do') and, less successfully, plugged away at his piano lessons, determined to pass his final LRSM (Licentiate of the Royal Schools of Music) examination. Ann remembers that he would play 'for relaxation' following breakfast most mornings at Dublin Street.

June of 2008 represented the last month of James's old life, the frenetic routine he had maintained for almost half a century. On the 15th he had attended a party to celebrate two hundred years of Heriot Row East, at which he read his own reminiscences, 'standing in the drawing-room of No. 17, where Gaga and Grandada sat 100 years ago'. And just over a week later, he attended a ceremony at the Middle Temple with the Queen and Duke of Edinburgh, the Duke being another figure who had loomed large in the latter period of his career.

Then occurred his second and final illness. James had undergone a biopsy a few months before, while in late June he also had tests on his kidneys, one of which was later removed. Basically, his cancer had returned, although this time chemotherapy proved unnecessary. On 7 July, he managed to convene a meeting of neighbours and officials to discuss the problem of student-generated noise on Dublin Street, while a serious burglary a couple of months later came at the worst possible time, upsetting him and Ann greatly.

In November 2008, James visited Parliament House, which had been the focus of his legal career for half a century (as well as his family for much longer than that), for the last time, being shown the new judge's library in which he looked up some references for a talk he was due to give the following week ('all quite a moving experience'), while a few days later Mungo Bovey, the Keeper of the Advocates' Library, came to Dublin Street to see 'the relics I have of Da's work on the Laigh and Parliament Halls'. There was an overwhelming sense that another era was drawing to a close.

In early 2009, James underwent a blood transfusion at the Western General Hospital, although when a scan revealed enlarged lymph nodes his diagnosis became much more serious. His son Tim visited Edinburgh on 17 January ('he is a tower of strength and so absolutely sensible'), shortly before his father marked his seventy-seventh birthday (although he felt 'an awful lot older'). Jamie had also come over from South Africa for his father's birthday on 29 January. James told him not only how much he loved his family but how determined he had been for his two sons to be given the freedom to forge their own paths in life.

The final entry in James's diary, a comprehensive record of his life he had maintained for more than sixty years, anticipated an operation on 3 February. 'Pray to the Lord', wrote James, 'that all will go well.'

His friend Sandy Wilkinson recalled that the outward courage with which James faced this new adversity 'flowed from strongly held Christian convictions nourished by the riches of Anglican spirituality and the sacramental life of the Church'. The Very Revd Dr Graham Forbes, Provost of St Mary's since 1990, also recalled that faced with another bout of illness his faith 'was a comfort to him'. He added:

> It was a quiet faith, though, it wasn't broadcast from the rooftops. It sounds like a cliché but it's also true: he was a quiet man of prayer. James was trusting, quietly trusting in his last days. Still with humour, still with

compassion, still with interest about what was going on around and about. He clearly valued highly Ann's support and love – that was love in the guts. That journey, the pair of them journeyed together.

On 6 March 2009, James died peacefully in his sleep at Edinburgh's Murrayfield Hospital. Close family attended a private funeral with a Requiem Mass at St James the Great Church in Dollar. En route to the burial, the coffin briefly visited the garden at Shiel, where the priest said prayers as James's favourite bird, the cock pheasant, coincidentally appeared on the lawn and a flock of geese flew poignantly overhead. He was then buried beside his mother and father in the churchyard at Crook of Devon, the village closest to Briglands.

A 'Service of Thanksgiving' at St Mary's Cathedral on 3 May was a fitting celebration of his life and character. The service (to a full congregation) was conducted by Graham Forbes, the Scottish Episcopal Church was represented by the Rt Revd Brian Smith (the Bishop of Edinburgh) and the Lord Speaker of the House of Lords by David Beamish, clerk assistant, with tributes from Jamie and Tim, and addresses by Kenny Cameron and Dr Judith McClure. Fittingly, it was also rich in music, particularly from James's favourite composer Elgar. The Cathedral Choir was conducted by Duncan Ferguson, the Orchestra of St Mary's Music School was directed by Francis Cummings, and Nicholas Wearne was the organist. There was also a Bach cello solo (Suite No. 1) played by Raim Koo and Beethoven's Tempest Piano Sonata played by Richard Beauchamp, James's teacher towards the end of his life, who told the congregation he was confident James would have passed his LRSM exam given more time.

Jamie Clyde, meanwhile, reminded friends and family that his father had been 'one half of a team'. 'For forty-six years,' he added, 'Ann was his sounding board, his rock and his soul mate. While many couples grow apart, as the years passed they grew closer and closer, creating such a stable and loving home for Tim and me.' By their own admission, only recently had James's sons come to appreciate the 'true value and importance' of their father's work, not least Jamie, who having lived in Africa, now appreciated the importance of a respected and independent judiciary. Like most children, they had lacked any alternative reference point, but later, as adults and fathers themselves, they realised (as Jamie put it) 'his brilliance in his patience, his constant encouragement, his ability to motivate, his enormous wealth of knowledge and his interest in whatever my interests happened to be at the time'.

It mattered little that James had not ended up following in the footsteps of his father and grandfather and become a Member of Parliament, Lord Advocate and ultimately Lord President, for with his formidable legal mind and acute sense of the role of the law in society he had – from the mid 1980s – followed his own path, distinct in achievements and positions held, yet at the same time firmly in the spirit of the first and second Lords Clyde. As James had once remarked, 'there is more in life than the law', and he had lived up to that by achieving as much outside a courtroom as he had at Parliament House, Westminster and in Northern Ireland. And if there was occasional self-doubt, it simply served to make him a better lawyer, a more sympathetic judge and, most importantly, a more rounded human being.

In his tribute to a friend since their days at the Edinburgh Academy, Kenny Cameron said he could do no better than to quote the writer Robert Louis Stevenson, another Academical, doyen of the Speculative Society and member of the Faculty of Advocates:

> That man is a success who has lived well, laughed often and loved much: who has gained the respect of intelligent men and the love of children: who has filled his niche and accomplished his task; who leaves the world better than he found it, whether by an improved

poppy, a perfect poem or a rescued soul: who never lacked appreciation of earth's beauty or failed to express it: who looked for the best in others and gave the best he had.

'All that James did,' concluded Cameron, 'and more.'

Those present that day at St Mary's Cathedral departed with an order of service which ended with some verse – a poetical epitaph – composed by James in the final weeks of his life:

> As I pass gently into history
> The past is present and the present past
> Time and eternity into one.
>
> But mourn no more for memory remains
> And that immortal essence which will be
> Support and comfort in your solitude.
>
> Think only gentle thoughts of me
> Forget the imperfections and forgive the wrongs
> Remember what you can until memories fade.
>
> May peace and joy stay vivid in your mind
> Faith is the guide whatever may befall
> And love is still the greatest memory of all.

Index